Saint Francis, Pope Francis

A Common Vision

Gina Loehr
with Al Giambrone

PUBLISHED BY FRANCISCAN MEDIA
Cincinnati, Ohio

Cover and book design by Mark Sullivan
Cover image © L'Osservatore Romano

Library of Congress Cataloging-in-Publication Data
Loehr, Gina.
St. Francis, Pope Francis : a common vision / Gina Loehr, with Al Giambrone.
pages cm
Includes bibliographical references.
ISBN 978-1-61636-747-3 (alk. paper)
1. Francis, of Assisi, Saint, 1182-1226. 2. Francis, Pope, 1936- I. Title.
BX4700.F6L63 2014
271'.302—dc23
2013045145
ISBN 978-1-61636-747-3

Published by Servant Books, an imprint of Franciscan Media.
28 W. Liberty St.
Cincinnati, OH 45202
www.FranciscanMedia.org

Printed in the United States of America.
Printed on acid-free paper.
14 15 16 17 18 5 4 3 2 1

For my husband, Joe
—G.L.
For my wife, Yvonne
—A.G.

And when the Lord gave me some brothers, no one showed me what I ought to do, but the Most High Himself revealed to me that I should live according to the form of the holy Gospel.[1]

—St. Francis

We are all invited to walk the streets of the world with our brothers and sisters, proclaiming and witnessing to our faith in Christ and making ourselves heralds of his Gospel.[2]

—Pope Francis

CONTENTS

FOREWORD

Fr. Jonathan Morris

From the day Jorge Mario Bergoglio from Buenos Aires was elected pope, he has caught the world's attention—first of all by taking the name Francis. In the short time he's been our 266th pope, he's become known as the "people's pope," and those people have coined the phrase "the Francis effect" to describe the impact he's had so far.

His popularity continues to grow. Every Wednesday he holds a papal audience in St. Peter's Square in Rome, and these draw more crowds than even John Paul II's. At World Youth Day in Brazil, three million people attended Mass on the Copacabana beach—many of them young people.

I travel extensively, and I've experienced the pope's international appeal. In airports, on the street, in restaurants, it's not uncommon for strangers to approach me to say, "Hey, Father, I like your pope!" or "This guy *gets* it!"

And he wants all of us to get it, too. Pope Francis wants everyone—Catholics, Christians, believers, and non-believers—to get back to the basics of faith. He demonstrates this for us by choosing to live very simply (making his home in the guest house rather than the papal apartment, for instance). He's even surprised many of the cardinals who elected him with his radical humility.

His simple teaching reaches people's hearts. Much like the example of his papal namesake, St. Francis of Assisi, Pope Francis tells us that, if we intend to follow Jesus, we must do it in a very sincere, simple way—one that communicates a very strong message. And his heartfelt words are not just meant for Catholics or Christians. Seekers are discovering a man who speaks to them, too—not saying, "Whatever you feel like doing is wonderful," but instead calling them to step up in a way they might not have considered before:

"How about taking care of the poor?"

"How about living a life of mission and purpose?"

"How about deciding you're going to live for others, not just for yourself?"

Jesus told St. Francis: "Francis, repair my Church which, as you can see, is falling into ruins." Today, Pope Francis is out to bring healing and hope to that same Church. To the priests and bishops, his message is clear: Don't just sit around in your rectories and parishes; say "no" to clericalism. It's not about your power, your authority…no, it's about service.

Pope Francis gives daily homilies, which can be found on the Vatican website. I'm struck as I listen to them by how down-to-earth and yet profound these are. Two examples illustrate what I mean. During one homily, he shared proof that you can't take material goods with you by saying, "Have you ever seen a moving van in a funeral procession?" In another, he mentioned that referring to God as "our Father" means that none of us are "only children."

St. Francis and Pope Francis do share a common vision: You can find meaning, purpose, and passion in life, and the way to do that is through friendship with God.

INTRODUCTION
Loving Christ, Living the Gospel

When he took the name Francis, our pope surprised the world. Everybody knows St. Francis of Assisi. Almost everybody loves him. But we didn't expect him to show up as a papal patron. It breaks the mold.

We have to stretch back to 1903 just to find a pope who wasn't a Benedict, a John, a Paul, or a Pius, and that only brings us to the thirteenth Leo. We haven't had a pope who was the first to use a name for exactly eleven hundred years. Thus the selection of the name Francis spoke volumes even before the new pontiff uttered a single word. This pope is going to be different.

Of course, every pope is different. Each brings to his pontificate a unique set of gifts and inclinations. Every one of them is charged with the same task—to be the pastor of the universal Church—but each does it in his own way. We must admit, however, that Pope Francis's particular style has intrigued people and captured their attention, even to the point of being named *TIME* magazine's Man of the Year in 2013. He hasn't reinvented the papacy, as some might have us believe. It's just that he's doing things with what we might call a twist.

That's what St. Francis did too. He, like all the saints before and since, loved Christ and lived the Gospel, but he did so in a way that got people's attention. And while it would be absurd to claim that Pope Francis is a mirror image of St. Francis, these men do share some significant things, not the least of which is the ability to remind people of the basic Gospel message.

St. Francis has already proven himself to be a genuine disciple of the Christian Gospel. He is enjoying the rewards of his labors even now, as he gazes on the face of God in heaven and prays for us on earth. The pope, on the other hand, is still on this side of the pearly gates. Although Jorge Mario Bergoglio has nearly eight decades of exemplary Christianity under his papal sash, he hasn't arrived yet. And he knows it. That's why he asked us to pray for him minutes after getting his new assignment. And that's why he has chosen a patron who can help keep him on the right track.

FOLLOWING ST. FRANCIS

In choosing St. Francis as his patron, our Holy Father indicated his desire to imitate the holy man from Assisi. And this is no small task! Some consider St. Francis to be the greatest saint in the history of Christianity.

Without a doubt, St. Francis loved Jesus with extraordinary zeal. He was dedicated to being an authentic image of Christ to the world. Hence the pope's choice to follow Francis is ultimately a choice to keep himself, and his authority, rooted firmly in Christ.

All the saints love Christ, to be sure, but what is noteworthy about St. Francis is his remarkable success at imitating Christ down to the details. As that pope from 1903, Leo XIII, wrote in his encyclical about Francis: "By his numerous virtues...and above all by his austerity of life, this irreproachable man endeavored to reproduce in himself the image of Christ Jesus."[3]

Clearly the endeavor went well. People saw in St. Francis a reflection of the Lord. And they liked what they saw. This is why folks flocked to Francis. This is why he inspired them and why his influence changed their lives.

St. Francis's popularity was a side effect of his authenticity. The man captivated people in his own day, and he continues to do so today. He is perhaps, of all the saints of the Catholic Church, the one who has most captured the attention, affection, and admiration of Catholics and non-Catholics alike.

This widespread fame of St. Francis has at times, however, run the risk of reducing him to a spiritual caricature or a holy cartoon. His cement likeness, complete with a sparrow on his shoulder and a squirrel at his feet, is often a focal point of bathtub grottos and quasi-religious peace gardens. But his spirituality is not a platitude set in plaster. Francis is a man whose faith was at once simple and profound.

What Francis did, he did simply out of love for Christ. His often unpredictable and sometimes extreme behavior was part of the love story. G.K. Chesterton explains the phenomenon well:

> But as St. Francis did not love humanity but men, so he did not love Christianity but Christ. Say, if you think so, that he was a lunatic loving an imaginary person; but an imaginary person, not an imaginary idea.... Tell it as the tale of one of the Troubadours, and the wild things he would do for his lady.... In such a romance there would be no contradiction between the poet gathering flowers in the sun and enduring a freezing vigil in the snow, between his praising all earthly and bodily beauty and then refusing to eat, and between his glorifying gold and purple and perversely going in rags, between his showing pathetically a hunger for a happy life and a thirst for a heroic death. All these riddles would easily be resolved in the simplicity of any noble love; only this was so noble a love that nine out of ten men have hardly even heard of it....

> To this great mystic his religion was not a thing like a
> theory but a thing like a love affair.[4]

Francis threw himself into the arms of Christ with the careless gusto of a man who is head over heels in love. There were no cautious calculations. There was no concern for what others might say. Francis just took Jesus at his word, believing what he promised and doing what he said. This we call Gospel simplicity. And Francis was a master of it.

Simple though it was, Francis's faith often manifested itself in extraordinary ways. Of all the dramatic moments in the life of this man, perhaps the one that most clearly indicates his whole-hearted dedication to the Gospel is the tale of his departure from his father's house. Having resolved to financially support the restoration of a certain church, the twenty-four-year-old Francis Bernardone sold some fabric from the shelves of his father, a cloth merchant, and applied the proceeds to the cause. When Pietro Bernardone learned of his son's thievery, well-intentioned though it was, he presented the matter to the courts. The ordeal became unpleasant and drawn out, and Francis went into hiding. When he emerged, he and his father came before the local bishop to resolve the dispute once and for all.

The resolution was an unexpected one. Francis stood before those gathered and declared, "Up to this time I have called Pietro Bernardone father, but now I am the servant of God. Not only the money but everything that can be called his I will restore to my father, even the very clothes he has given me."[5]

Then the holy thief stripped himself down to his last layer, piled his garments at the feet of Pietro, and crowned them with every bit of money he had. He asked the blessing of the bishop and walked away into the snowy forest. And there—freezing, half naked, and alone without possessions or parents—Francis began to sing.

For St. Francis, casting off the expectations of society and the burden of wealth was a true liberation. He wasn't worried about the consequences of his choice. He trusted in Christ, who promised that "every one who has left houses or brothers or sisters or father or mother or children or fields, for my name's sake, will receive a hundredfold, and inherit eternal life" (Matthew 19:29). Yes, St. Francis took this statement literally, as he was like to do with all of Christ's words. He lived as if Jesus meant what he said, rather than treating the Gospel as merely a poetic suggestion to be admired and then ignored.

This simple faith should not be so radical. But alas, we are so often paralyzed by our fears that we stop short of truly heeding the Gospel. Francis startles and refreshes us because he wasn't afraid. He embraced the Gospel with complete courage and confidence. And people took notice.

EMBRACING GOSPEL VALUES

At a time in history when abuse and corruption had distorted much Christian practice, God raised up St. Francis. He was a living reminder of the fundamental Gospel values that Jesus had practiced and preached a millennium before. As Pope Leo XIII noted, God gave Francis the special grace "of inciting Christians to virtue, and of bringing back to the imitation of Christ those men who had strayed both long and far."[6] Then-Archbishop Bergoglio also praised the saint of Assisi because "he brought to Christianity an idea of poverty against the luxury, pride, vanity of the civil and ecclesiastical powers of the time. He changed history."[7]

Now, nearly a millennium after St. Francis gave his witness, God appears to be giving us another reminder. He has raised up Pope Francis in this era in which so many people have succumbed to being merely cultural Christians, idly practicing the rituals of religion without embracing the fullness of the Gospel message. Not surprisingly, secular society is less and less compelled by this hollow Christianity. Thus the pope insists, "The proposal of the Gospel must be more simple, profound, radiant."[8] He is reminding us not to be satisfied with the empty witness of Christianity half lived. At this time in history, we need to remind the world of what Pope Francis calls "the freshness and fragrance of the Gospel."[9]

The Church stands to benefit from Pope Francis's perspective. Even now the Catholic Church is suffering from a tragic internal tension between so-called liberals and conservatives. These labels emerge in large part because of our failure to follow the Gospel in its entirety. Perhaps we have great reverence for the sacraments Christ instituted but fail to express any tangible concern for the poor whom he loved. Or conversely, we might emphasize reaching out in Christlike compassion but balk when it comes to heeding the authority of the Church Christ established.

In the midst of such dichotomies, Pope Francis seeks to strike a balance. Like St. Francis, he is trying to do what the Gospel commands. And again like his namesake, he doesn't seem to mind if he makes people a little uncomfortable in the process. After all, Christ had that effect too. As Cardinal Timothy Dolan put it:

> I find [Pope Francis] a challenge...in a good way, like Jesus
> is a challenge. He's saying to me and I think everybody else
> in the world, "Let's reexamine our approach to things. Let's

examine if we are faithful to the teaching of Jesus, especially when it comes to love, joy, hope, and mercy."[10]

Indeed, as individuals and as a Church, we can only make progress when we are truly faithful to Christ. Pope Francis understands this. After his election to the papacy, he gave a beautiful description of the role of the pope in relation to Christ:

> Christ is the Church's Pastor, but his presence in history passes through the freedom of human beings; from their midst one is chosen to serve as his Vicar, the Successor of the Apostle Peter. Yet Christ remains the centre, not the Successor of Peter: Christ, Christ is the centre. Christ is the fundamental point of reference, the heart of the Church. Without him, Peter and the Church would not exist or have reason to exist.[11]

This is something the new pontiff takes seriously. He wants to fulfill his role with dedication to Christ as his primary task. He has asked for prayers to this effect. "I ask you for a special prayer for me," he said in an address to representatives of churches and world religions, "so that I can be a pastor according to the heart of Christ."[12]

To act according to the heart of Christ means to embrace the priorities that Christ embraced. It means living according to the values of the Gospel he preached, values that stand in stark contrast to much of what surrounds us in this day and age. As Christians we are called to transform the world instead of letting the world transform us.

Pope Francis has reflected on this in terms of a spiritual battle. In a retreat he gave for the bishops of Spain, then-Cardinal Bergoglio asked:

What is at stake in this war? It is whether in my heart, as well as in the heart of the Church and of humanity itself, the Kingdom of Heaven will be established, with his law of love and the Lord's way of life: poverty, humility, and service. Or whether the kingdom of this world will triumph, with its laws and values of wealth, vanity, and pride.[13]

Like St. Francis before him, Pope Francis wants to follow the Lord's way of life by imitating Christ's in his *humility*, his *charity*, his love for the *Church*, his *peace*, and his *joy*. In this book we will see how the humility of both men manifests itself in poverty and service; how their charity extends to the needy and to the downtrodden; how they love the Church both in her authority and in her members who constitute the body of Christ; how the peace in their hearts helps encourage peace among their neighbors; and how they have found joy both in the cross and in the kingdom of God.

Of course, we cannot reduce the Gospel or the depth of the Francises' faith to a few handy categories. But these five major themes emerge consistently when we consider the lives, teachings, and writings of these particular men. And this should come as no surprise; both St. Francis and Pope Francis seek to imitate Christ, who emphasized these values in his life and teachings.

Rather than make a simple biographical comparison between the two Francises, this book will consider how these men have each, in his own way, embraced the common vision of loving Christ and living the Gospel. Thus we begin each chapter with quotes from the two Francises, followed by a look at what Jesus taught us about the Gospel value we are considering. Then we give examples of how St. Francis and Pope Francis have demonstrated commitment to that value.

Finally we pause to examine what we can learn from the Francises, because in truth, these Gospel values are not just for canonized saints and popes. Jesus calls us *all* to humility and charity. He has given us *all* the benefit of the Church, and he offers *every one of us* peace and joy. Thus, each chapter concludes with a related teaching from the Church and some questions to help us discern how we can incorporate these values into our lives as the people of God.

CHAPTER ONE
Humility

Consider, brothers, the humility of God and "pour out your
hearts before Him," and be ye humbled that ye may be
exalted by Him.[14]

—St. Francis

So it is always with God's love, that, in order to reach us,
takes the way of humility.... One can take no other road, if
I do not lower myself, if you do not lower yourself, you are
not a Christian.[15]

—Pope Francis

The Francises are in good company when they extol the virtue
of humility. Countless saints and theologians throughout history
have, ironically, showered a great deal of praise on humility. St.
Augustine called it the foundation of all other virtues and taught
that no one can reach the kingdom of heaven without it. St.
Vincent de Paul believed humility to be the most powerful weapon
for overcoming the devil. And Teresa of Avila insisted that a little
study of humility was more valuable than all the knowledge in
the world.

Even without such a distinguished cheering section, humility
would remain essential to the Christian life. Those who seek to
imitate Christ recognize that he is a model of this virtue. From the
instant of his incarnation in the womb of a poor maiden to the
moment of his death on the cross, Jesus illustrates his willingness
to be lowly in the eyes of the world. As we read in the letter to the

Philippians, "Being found in human form he humbled himself and became obedient unto death, even death on a cross" (2:8).

But Jesus gave us more than an example of being humble. He also spoke clearly about the value of embracing this virtue. In Matthew's Gospel he says, "Whoever exalts himself will be humbled, and whoever humbles himself will be exalted" (Matthew 23:12). This counterintuitive theme reappears several times throughout the Gospels, including two repetitions of exactly the same wording in the Gospel of Luke.

It also resonates in the similar formula "Whoever would save his life will lose it; and whoever loses his life for my sake and the gospel's will save it" (Mark 8:35). This too is an important teaching that Matthew's and Luke's Gospels record in nearly identical fashion. When taken in tandem, these teachings indicate that humility *for the sake of Christ* is a foundation for the fullness of life. Indeed, the humbler we are, the greater we are. For as Jesus said, "Whoever humbles himself like [a] child, he is the greatest in the kingdom of heaven" (Matthew 18:4).

The early Church recognized the centrality of Christ's teaching on humility and preserved the idea in the biblical epistles. The letter of James slightly reformulates the words of Christ, saying, "Humble yourselves before the Lord and he will exalt you" (James 4:10), and emphasizes that "God opposes the proud, but gives grace to the humble" (James 4:6). The first letter of St. Peter adds the exhortation "Clothe yourselves, all of you, with humility toward one another" (1 Peter 5:5). This epistle also reiterates the original theme: "Humble yourselves therefore under the mighty hand of God, that in due time he may exalt you" (1 Peter 5:6). And the letter to the Philippians instructs us to "do nothing from selfishness or conceit, but in humility count others better than yourselves" (Philippians 2:3).

St. Francis and Pope Francis, in their dedication to authentic Gospel values, both emphasize the importance of humility. For these men the virtue manifests itself in two particularly striking ways.

First, through poverty. Both Francises recognize that an undeniable aspect of Christ's humility was the fact that he was poor. He was born in the lowliest of physical conditions to poor parents. Even during the years of his public ministry, when his popularity was at a height, Jesus never garnered for himself the comforts of wealth. "Foxes have holes, and birds of the air have nests," he once said, "but the Son of man has nowhere to lay his head" (Matthew 8:20).

Jesus expected his disciples to be poor by choice. To the young man who sought perfection, Jesus said, "If you would be perfect, go, sell what you possess and give to the poor, and you will have treasure in heaven; and come, follow me" (Matthew 19:21). When he sent his disciples out to preach the Gospel, he instructed them in the ways of poverty: "Carry no purse, no bag, no sandals" (Luke 10:4). And he taught the value of shifting our focus from material to spiritual wealth when he told his followers, "Sell your possessions, and give alms; provide yourselves with purses that do not grow old, with a treasure in the heavens that does not fail, where no thief approaches and no moth destroys. For where your treasure is, there will your heart be also" (Luke 12:33–34).

Jesus emphasized the interior nature of poverty as well. Having few possessions means little if it brings with it an attitude of bitterness or envy. Rather, Jesus said, "Blessed are the poor in spirit, for theirs is the kingdom of heaven" (Matthew 5:3). Christian poverty goes beyond a catalog of what we do or do not own. It extends to our spirit of possessiveness in general. Thus poverty includes giving up the quest to possess honors and prestige.

Alongside poverty, Jesus also reveals the virtue of humility through servant leadership. He told his disciples, "He who is greatest among you shall be your servant" (Matthew 23:11). And he practiced what he preached.

The foremost example of this comes from the night of the Last Supper, when Jesus washed the feet of his disciples. After bending down to carry out this lowly task, Jesus explained himself:

> Do you know what I have done to you? You call me Teacher and Lord; and you are right, for so I am. If I then, your Lord and Teacher, have washed your feet, you also ought to wash one another's feet. For I have given you an example, that you also should do as I have done to you. (John 13:12–15)

The concept of humility itself can feel abstract or intangible, but the specific practices of poverty and servant leadership give substance to this virtue. As we turn now to the lives and writings of St. Francis and Pope Francis, we will see concrete examples of how to embrace the Gospel value of humility.

ST. FRANCIS AND POVERTY

Known sometimes simply as the *Poverello* or the "little poor man," St. Francis's devotion to the humble practice of poverty is a trademark of his particular brand of holiness. For him, loving the poor and serving them were not enough. He had to be poor. But even that was not enough. He wanted to be poor just as Christ was poor, confidently entrusting his life to the care of his heavenly Father.

Unlike Christ, however, Francis did not begin his life in poverty. Born into the successful Bernardone family in the year 1181, Francis grew up with every material comfort. During his youth he enjoyed parading around his hometown of Assisi, Italy, in fine clothes while spending his parents' money on his friends' entertainment. His mother even remarked that her child seemed more like a prince than a merchant's son. But Francis eventually abandoned this love for worldly wealth.

One of the earliest manifestations of St. Francis's desire for Christian poverty took place one day as he was returning to Assisi after selling his father's cloth in a nearby town. With his heart fresh with the love of God, Francis was overcome with a feeling of burden from the money in his pocket. So he determined to get rid of it.

Coming upon the dilapidated Church of St. Damien, Francis entered and found the priest. He kissed the pastor's hands and offered him the money. This came as a shock to the priest, who knew Francis as a shallow and foolish youth, and he refused the money that rightfully belonged to Francis's father. Francis, however, threw the money on the windowsill. His growing desire was to seek only the treasure of heaven.

This inclination to be free from the goods of the earth was soon confirmed in Francis's soul, most likely on February 24 of the year 1208. That day he heard the Gospel reading that inspired his lifelong devotion to the ideal he referred to as Lady Poverty: "You received without pay; give without pay. Take no gold, nor silver, nor copper in your belts, no bag for your journey, nor two tunics, nor sandals, nor a staff" (Matthew 10:8–10). Upon hearing this reading, Francis cried out, "This is what I wish, this is what I seek, this is what I long to do with all my heart."[16] Then he took the shoes off his feet and traded his belt for the simple knotted rope that was destined to become the symbol of the Franciscan habit.

This passionate resolution was not a passing fancy. The men who eventually began to follow Francis drew near to him in part because of his radical adherence to Gospel poverty. The path they chose was not easy, nor was it left up to chance or personal inclination. Francis clearly articulated his austere expectations in the words of his First Rule:

> The friars who have already made their profession of obedience may have one habit with a hood and, if necessary, another without a hood. They may also have a cord and trousers. All the friars must wear poor clothes and they can patch them with pieces of sackcloth and other material, with God's blessing.[17]

Not only was the wardrobe sparse, but any other personal possessions were out of the question. Indeed, Francis preached a disregard for money itself in a later chapter of this same rule:

> And so all the friars, no matter where they are or where they go, are forbidden to take or accept money in any way or under any form, or have it accepted for them, for clothing or books, or as wages, or in any other necessity, except to provide for the urgent needs of those who are ill. We should have no more use or regard for money in any of its forms than for dust.[18]

Even in the face of these strict constraints, the community called the Friars Minor grew, and humble simplicity remained a hallmark of their charism.

On one occasion, however, Francis returned from a journey and was shocked to find a small stone building erected outside the brothers' headquarters, at the small chapel near St. Mary of the Angels in Assisi known as the Portiuncula. The new structure was occupied by some of the friars. Because owning such an edifice was in stark contrast to perfect poverty, Francis took it upon himself to ascend to the roof of the building and begin tearing off the shingles. At the urging of his companions, he ceased his deconstruction but cried out to them,

> Brothers, brothers, the way that I have entered is one of humility and simplicity! If it is a new way know that it was taught to me by God Himself, and that I will follow no other.... The Lord wishes me to be a new kind of fool in the world, and will not lead me by any other way.[19]

Before he died, Francis gave final instructions that must have been motivated in part by the recollection of this unfortunate scene. Dictating his last exhortations concerning poverty, he said,

> The friars must be very careful not to accept churches or poor dwellings for themselves, or anything else built for them, unless they are in harmony with poverty which we have promised in the Rule; and they should occupy these places only as strangers or pilgrims.[20]

Even when the order, which grew rapidly during Francis's life, would gather at their triennial chapter meeting, Francis insisted on maintaining their austere lifestyle. When, in the year 1221, some five thousand men gathered for the assembly, no house of hospitality was in sight, and not even a tent was pitched. Instead the congregation of mendicants slept outdoors on the ground, the only accommodations being a piece of wood or stone for a pillow and the option of a straw mat upon which to recline. Hence the meeting earned the title "The Chapter of Mats."

Other provisions were also left in the hands of God during this event. Francis and his brothers assigned no cook from their midst and didn't spend a minute searching for food to feed the multitude. Rather, Francis preached about the humility and poverty taught by the Gospel and instructed his men to "be diligent in prayer and praise to God without care for your bodily nourishment, for Christ has expressly promised to provide for you."[21] The men listened to his sermon and obeyed, going off to pray.

According to tradition, St. Dominic was in attendance at the chapter meeting, and he questioned the prudence of taking no consideration for the needs of these thousands of hungry men. But his question was resolved when a long procession of townsfolk suddenly appeared. In honor of their beloved local saint and his poor friars, they brought donkeys loaded with beans, cheese, bread, and wine. All ate and were satisfied. As the story goes, Dominic resolved to observe evangelical poverty and to make it the practice of the sons of his order as well.

POPE FRANCIS AND POVERTY

"My people are poor and I am one of them."[22] So Pope Francis replied when questioned about his austere lifestyle. Indeed, Jorge Mario Bergoglio has never been one to shun either the people who live in poverty or the experience of poverty itself.

Pope Francis did not grow up in poverty, but neither did materialism afflict his childhood. He was the eldest of five children of unassuming Italian immigrants. His father was an accountant for the Argentine railroad; his mother stayed at home, overseeing a modest and frugal domestic existence.

The Bergoglios considered themselves fortunate to have food, clothing, and housing. Yet they never owned a car and never took a vacation. The children grew up appreciating material security rather than taking it for granted. They did not leave food on their plates, and new clothes were considered an extravagance. This laid a foundation of compassion and empathy for those without the benefit of material security.

Jorge's father believed in learning the value of work at an early age, so at his insistence Jorge got a factory job when he turned thirteen. To this day he remains grateful to his father for instilling in him a sense of the dignity of work. And what dignified work was in store for Jorge!

Upon his election as the leader of the world's 1.2 billion Roman Catholics, there was little known and much to be learned about Cardinal Bergoglio. But very quickly, observers recognized him as a man of striking humility manifested in his love for the poor and his personal practice of poverty.

One of the initial hints of this humility came when he appeared on the balcony of St. Peter's in his plain white cassock rather than the traditional ermine-trimmed red mozetta cloak. He wore his simple black shoes instead of the customary red papal loafers. (The black pair was a gift from friends in Buenos Aires who were embarrassed to send their cardinal off to the papal conclave in the tattered old shoes he had been wearing.)

After his appearance to the crowds, the new pope declined the car and driver that awaited him in favor of riding the shuttle bus with his brother cardinals back to the Domus Sanctae Marthae, where they had all been housed during the conclave. The next day, in the early morning hours, he quietly slipped out of the Vatican in a Volkswagen instead of a Mercedes to pay homage to the Virgin Mother at St. Mary Major.

Even the *New York Times* noticed these signs of humility: "[Francis] wore simple black shoes and an ordinary wristwatch with a thick black band to his first Mass as pontiff…. In an ancient institution where style often translates into substance, Francis, in his first 24 hours as Pope, has dramatically shifted the tone of the papacy."[23]

But the very first and perhaps most telling sign of this pope's humble devotion to poverty was his choice of a name. He chose Francis. He explained his decision in a meeting with members of the press on the third day after his election:

> During the election, I was seated next to the Archbishop Emeritus of São Paolo and Prefect Emeritus of the Congregation for the Clergy, Cardinal Claudio Hummes: a good friend, a good friend! When things were looking dangerous, he encouraged me. And when the votes reached two thirds, there was the usual applause, because the Pope had been elected. And he gave me a hug and a kiss, and said: "Don't forget the poor!" And those words came to me: the poor, the poor. Then, right away, thinking of the poor, I thought of Francis of Assisi. Then I thought of all the wars, as the votes were still being counted, till the end. Francis is also the man of peace. That is how the name came into my heart: Francis of Assisi. For me, he is the man of poverty, the man of peace…. How I would like a Church which is poor and for the poor![24]

When he stepped into his new position, not typically associated with the practice of poverty, Pope Francis tied a little white string around the finger of his entire pontificate; he established a perpetual reminder of his commitment to poverty, in the form of his own name. With every "Pope Francis" he will recall the *Poverello*.

As stories quickly revealed, this wasn't a show. The man had been poor and humble for a long time. Upon his appointment as archbishop of Buenos Aires in 1998, for example, Bergoglio chose to live in a small apartment on the second floor of the curia building instead of taking up residence in the grand home customarily reserved for the archbishop. He declined a personal staff, preferring to cook his own meals and rarely dining out or going to parties. He kept track of all his appointments himself, in a small black spiral notebook that he carried in his pocket.

The tales of his simplicity go on. Upon his elevation to the rank of cardinal in 2001, Bergoglio had his predecessor's robes altered to fit him. Instead of using a limousine or even a taxi when he went to the cathedral or out into the city to tend his flock, he rode the bus or the subway dressed as a simple priest. For travel abroad he flew economy class.

On one occasion, on his way to visit a parish in a poor neighborhood, Fr. Jorge (as the archbishop preferred to be called) rode the bus as usual. Later in the evening, a bricklayer stood before him and said with emotion, "I am proud of you, because when I came here with my companions on the bus, I saw you sitting in one of the last seats, like one of us. I told them it was you, but no one believed me."[25]

These and similar stories have captivated the attention of countless people since the moment we heard the words *Habemus Papam!* Indeed, Pope Francis has gained the world's attention, even its admiration, through his humble, voluntary poverty.

For Pope Francis, as for St. Francis, poverty was a choice. It was a choice he made when he entered the Society of Jesus—the Jesuits—founded by St. Ignatius of Loyola (whose conversion, by the way, was inspired by the example of St. Francis). On April 22, 1973, Jorge Bergoglio made his perpetual vows, promising to live a life of poverty and also vowing not to consent to any mitigation of the society's observance of poverty. This is a choice he continues to make, even as the opportunity and temptation to do otherwise are ever present. He not only stands in solidarity with the poor whom he loves and serves; he also imitates the poverty of Christ himself.

St. Francis and Servant Leadership

Long before "servant leadership" was a catch phrase in Christian circles, St. Francis was a leader who served his followers. And he had many of them. The way people flocked to Francis, he could have easily surrounded himself with an entourage of assistants to pave the road he traveled. But consistent with his devotion to the Gospel and the example of Christ, he deliberately remained a humble servant. He did not use his influence to manipulate or coerce others but always tried to lead by example and avoid any abuse of leadership. He wrote in his Rule:

> All the friars without exception are forbidden to wield power or authority, particularly over one another. Our Lord tells us in the Gospel that *the rulers of the Gentiles lord it*

over them, and their great men exercise authority over them (Matthew 20:25). That is not to be the way among the friars. Among them *whoever wishes to become great shall be* their *servant, and whoever wishes to be first shall be* their minister (Matthew 20:26–27), and he is their servant. *Let him who is the greatest among you become as the youngest* (Luke 22:26).[26]

As with poverty, Francis clearly expected those who joined the band of brothers to embrace the spirit of humble service. Even the use of titles was affected by the principle of safeguarding humility. Francis desired that "no one...be called 'Prior.' They are all to be known as 'Friars Minor' without distinction, and they should be prepared to wash one another's feet."[27]

The name "Friars Minor," or "Little Brothers," was a deliberate association with the lower class in the town of Assisi. The *majores* were the nobles, knights, and lords, while the *minores* were the common people. Francis chose to identify himself and his associates with those in the lower class. Most of the first twelve followers of Francis, in fact, were well-to-do citizens of Assisi; they were thus *majores* seeking to become *minores* in a true spirit of humility.

Though certain men did exercise leadership roles to enable the work of the order, Francis desired that they carry out these positions with a spirit of service. He referred to them by the humble title of "ministers," and he spelled out in his First Rule that the friars who were elected ministers were "therefore servants of the other friars" and that "the ministers who are servants should remember the words of our Lord, *'The Son of Man has not come to be served but to serve'* (Matthew 20:28)."[28]

To ensure that those in positions of authority used their power for the good of others, Francis put in place a structure to hold the leaders accountable. He wrote that the friars "should examine the behavior of their ministers and servants in the light of reason and in a spirit of charity."[29] The encouragement of fraternal correction was meant to foster an atmosphere of genuine service. No one was to become so powerful that he was immune to correction and redirection when necessary.

This willingness to be corrected was central to Francis's own spirituality. In *The Little Flowers of St. Francis*, for example, we read an exchange with Brother Bernard, who failed to come when Francis called. Francis grew frustrated, but then he realized that Bernard had been praying. Francis reproved himself for expecting Bernard to come immediately. He lay on the ground before Bernard and instructed him to say, "Be humbled, thou son of Peter Bernardone, for thou art but a vile wretch; how camest thou to be so proud!"[30] Other such stories abound.

Along with embracing mutual correction, Francis also understood that a true servant leader must be willing to walk the same path that he directs others to follow. On one occasion he called upon Brother Rufino to go to Assisi and preach to the people there whatever God would direct him to say. Although Rufino was from one of the noblest families of the town, he was not gifted with preaching and struggled with the courage to do it. Pleading to be excused from the assignment, he reminded Francis of his simplicity and ignorance. But Francis did not excuse him. On the contrary, he directed the good brother to go and preach wearing just his breeches, as punishment for his failure to obey immediately!

Rufino was both humble and obedient, so he proceeded into town, entered the church, walked up to the altar, and began to preach *sine habitus*, amid the laughter of children and the ridicule of adults. Meanwhile St. Francis began to ask himself how he could order one of the noblest citizens of Assisi to preach to the people in such a state, like a madman. He said to himself, "By God, I am going to see to it that you yourself experience what you order others to do."

As any good servant leader would do, Francis faced up to the challenge of his own demands. He removed his habit, went to town, and entered the church where Rufino was preaching. Thus both men endured the ridicule of the town, which now doubled at the presence of two apparent lunatics.

When Brother Rufino concluded his remarks, Francis took to the pulpit and preached eloquently about penance, poverty, and the nakedness and humiliations of Christ. In the end the crowd was moved to tears by the courage of the humble brothers. Many wept so heartily over the passion of Christ that Rufino and Francis had to console and bless them before donning their habits and returning home praising God. [31]

POPE FRANCIS AND SERVANT LEADERSHIP

After a member of the Jesuits has professed his perpetual vows, he takes five additional simple vows. One of these involves a promise "never to 'strive or ambition' for any dignity in the church, like becoming a bishop."[32] This means that Jorge Mario Bergoglio— the bishop, the cardinal, the pope—took a vow not to seek any of these offices. Unlike perhaps all of the dignitaries and world leaders with whom he must engage, the role he plays is not one he has desired, prepared for, or pursued.

The pope laughingly told a little girl who asked if he wanted to be pope: "No, I didn't want to become pope."[33] He explained to her that anyone who wants to be pope doesn't know what is in his best interest. This is a role that has been thrust upon him. It is a role he embraces because he has accepted God's calling, not because he thought himself equipped for the job.

As he humbly said to the cardinals when they elected him, "I am a sinner, but I trust in the infinite mercy and patience of our Lord Jesus Christ, and I accept in a spirit of penance."[34] Even as he carries out this task to lead the largest and oldest institution in the world, he plays the role of a servant, a role that he does desire, has prepared for, and pursues daily.

On Tuesday, March 19, 2013, the solemnity of St. Joseph, a ring with the image of St. Peter holding the keys of the kingdom was placed on the finger of Pope Francis, and the pallium was laid upon his shoulders as a sign of his authority. Six cardinals, representing the entire College of Cardinals, offered their obedience to him. Even as he was being appointed the most powerful man in the Church and one of the most powerful men in the world, he clearly laid out his vision of servant leadership. During the celebration of his inaugural Mass, he said:

> Today, together with the feast of St. Joseph, we are celebrating the beginning of the ministry of the new Bishop of Rome, the Successor of Peter, which also involves a certain power. Certainly, Jesus Christ conferred power upon Peter, but what sort of power was it? Jesus' three questions to Peter about love are followed by three commands: feed my lambs, feed my sheep.

Let us never forget that authentic power is service, and that the pope too, when exercising power, must enter ever more fully into that service which has its radiant culmination in the Cross. He must be inspired by the lowly, concrete and faithful service which marked St. Joseph and, like him, he must open his arms to protect all of God's people and embrace with tender affection the whole of humanity, especially the poorest, the weakest, the least important.[35]

The references to lowly, concrete, and faithful service were not idealistic, empty words. Pope Francis was describing a life of servant leadership that he was already living. For example, only three months after taking his final vows as a Jesuit, Fr. Bergoglio was elected provincial, the top post of the order in Argentina. But six years later he returned as rector to the seminary at San Miguel. This was, in effect, a self-imposed demotion. Then, as rector, he took on the task of cooking for the students. This would be like the governor of the state taking a job as a school principal and then spending his afternoons working in the school cafeteria.

Later, as archbishop and cardinal of Buenos Aires, Bergoglio was very committed to serving the priests of the archdiocese. He was known to cook for his priests from time to time, and he was available to them every day. Each morning he set aside one hour just to take calls from his priests on a cell phone reserved for them. And his priests numbered nearly four thousand!

Upon his rise to the See of Peter, humble gestures of servant leadership swiftly became a hallmark of his papacy. Just after the election, he politely stepped aside from the receiving line of Vatican officials to greet the regular folks who had been waiting for hours outside. His first words to the faithful gathered in St.

Peter's Square and around the world were "Brothers and sisters." Then, after offering a prayer for his predecessor, he humbly bowed before them and asked for their prayers. The entire square fell silent in a most extraordinary moment.

The day after his election, in his Mass for the Church with all the cardinal electors, Pope Francis walked to the ambo to deliver his homily instead of delivering it from his chair, as is customary for a pope. On his second full day on the job, the pope traveled secretly, in an unmarked car and without a large entourage, to a Roman hospital to visit Cardinal Jorge Mejia, who had suffered a heart attack during the conclave. After the half-hour visit he stopped to pray in the chapel with the thirteen nuns who work in the hospital, making a point afterward to individually greet them and others who were in the chapel.

Francis quickly shunned the traditional throne often used by popes in meetings with religious leaders and diplomats. He preferred to use an ordinary chair, not on a raised platform but on the same level as everyone else. A few days after his election, he met with Pope Emeritus Benedict at Castel Gondolfo. When the two men went into the chapel to pray, the pope emeritus offered the place of honor to the pope, but Francis declined. He wanted them to kneel together in the same pew, saying, "We are brothers."[36]

And then there were the phone calls. The pope's spirit of service is apparent in the priority he has made of reaching out to ordinary people. Following his election, he called his sister to say that he was all right, but she was so overwhelmed that she couldn't say anything. "He just kept repeating, 'Don't worry, I'm fine, pray for me,'"[37] she reported later. He said he wouldn't be calling the rest of the family because he didn't want to run up the Vatican phone bill.

He proceeded to call the Father General of the Jesuit order, but the doorman answered:

> "Good morning, it's Pope Francis, I'd like to speak with the Father General."
>
> "May I ask who's calling?" The Pope realized the young Italian man didn't believe it was him, so he kindly repeated.
>
> "Seriously, it's Pope Francis. What's your name?"
>
> "My name is Andrew."
>
> "How are you, Andrew?" asked the Pope.
>
> "Fine, pardon me, just a little bit confused."
>
> The Holy Father responded, "Don't worry, could you please connect me with the Father General? I would like to thank him for the beautiful letter he sent me."
>
> "Pardon me, Your Holiness, I'll connect you right now," said the doorman.
>
> "No problem. I'll wait as long as necessary."[38]

Thus said the most powerful religious leader in the world.

When he called the archdiocese of Buenos Aires to check in, a nun answered the phone and asked, "Who is calling?"

"Fr. Jorge," he said.

"Your Holiness?" she replied in shock.

"Oh, c'mon, it's Fr. Jorge," said the pope.[39]

He called his dentist in Argentina to cancel his appointments. He called a kiosk owner in Buenos Aires to say he wouldn't need a newspaper delivered anymore. He called his shoemaker in Argentina. He also called a woman who wrote him seeking help after being raped twice and an Italian man struggling to forgive God after the murder of his brother.

On the day of his inaugural Mass, he did not forget the thousands of his people back in the main square of Buenos Aires, spending the night there awaiting the Mass on television. At 3:32 A.M. they heard the voice of their former cardinal. He had called the cell phone of the rector of the cathedral, who was able to patch the call through the speakers set up outside the cathedral.

> Dear sons and daughters, I know you have gathered in the square. I know that you are saying prayers, I need them very much. We all walk united. We take care of each other, and continue to pray for me. To pray is so beautiful. It means looking to heaven and to our heart. We know that we have a good Father who is God.[40]

From his words as well as his actions, it is clear that servant leadership will be a central theme of Pope Francis's papacy. In a homily at the Metropolitan Cathedral in 2001 he said, "Power is but service. Power only makes sense if it is in service of the common good."[41] And in an interview on the topic of education, Cardinal Bergoglio captured the essence of servant leadership:

> Authority comes from the Latin *augere,* meaning "to make grow." To have authority is not to be an oppressor. Oppression is a distortion of authority. When exercised correctly, authority implies creating a space where a person can grow. Anyone with authority is capable of creating space to grow....
>
> [The word *authority*] has become synonymous with "I'm in charge here."...
>
> [But] having the "upper hand" doesn't mean to order and impose; it means to serve.[42]

Ultimately servant leadership is modeled after the leadership of the Lord. Pope Francis serves because it is what Jesus told us to do. Then-Cardinal Bergoglio once noted, "Jesus says that the one who rules must be like a servant.... The true power of religious leadership comes from service."[43] And in a homily at daily Mass on May 21, 2013, Pope Francis said:

> Real power is found in service. Just like Jesus, who didn't come to be served, but to serve. His service was seen on the Cross. He humbled Himself unto death, He died on a Cross for us, to serve us, to save us. It's with this path that the Church moves forward. For the Christian, getting ahead, progress, means humbling oneself. If we do not learn this Christian rule, we will never, ever be able to understand Jesus' true message on power.[44]

FOR REFLECTION: HOW WILL I RESPOND?

Catechism of the Catholic Church 520: "In all of his life Jesus presents himself as our model. He is 'the perfect man,' who invites us to become his disciples and follow him. In humbling himself, he has given us an example to imitate, through his prayer he draws us to pray, and by his poverty he calls us to accept freely the privation and persecutions that may come our way."

Consider: Where could I grow in the imitation of Christ's humility? What elements of his humility do I like to follow? What elements do I ignore or avoid?

* * *

St. Francis loved poverty. He personified the virtue using the endearing terms of a spouse, his "Lady Poverty," and was devoted to her. Through this devotion, he found liberation. Because he was unburdened by material attachments, he was free to follow Christ without reservation.

Consider: How do I feel about the practice of poverty in my own life? Have my material possessions ever restricted my freedom to follow Christ? If so, what am I especially attached to? How could detachment from these things enable me to better follow Christ's example?

• • •

Pope Francis is one of the most important and influential people in the world. Not only Catholics but people of many faiths look to him for leadership. Yet he insists that "authentic power is service." This perspective runs contrary to most worldly views of power. But it follows the model of Christ, who came "not to be served, but to serve."

Consider: What are my views about power? When have I had positions of leadership—in my family, my school, my workplace, my parish, or my community? How did I carry out these roles of power? Have I been a servant to those I lead?

CHAPTER TWO
Charity

Though I should speak with the tongue of men and of angels, and have not charity, nor show to my neighbor an example of virtue, I should be of little service to him, and none to myself.[45]

—St. Francis of Assisi

May you always be attentive to charity. Each individual Christian and every community is missionary to the extent that they bring to others and live the Gospel, and testify to God's love for all, especially those experiencing difficulties. Be missionaries of God's love and tenderness![46]

—Pope Francis

Without a doubt the Francises are both men of action. Each is rooted deeply in love for Christ and committed to a prayerful life, yet their spiritualities revolve around putting the Gospel into practice. St. Francis did spend some months in hermitlike solitude at the beginning of his conversion and toward the end of his life, but the vast majority of his time was dedicated to serving others for the love of God. Pope Francis too, although well aware of the importance of contemplation, has indicated time and again his commitment to getting out among the people and engaging in tangible acts of charity for those in need. The Francises model for us the active love—the *caritas*—of Christ.

During the years of his public ministry, Jesus taught and prayed, but he also engaged in acts of charity. He did this in two ways:

first, by ministering to people's physical needs. His miracles, for example, were directed primarily toward the needy. Jesus did not utilize his divine power to make the sun stand still, to part the waters, or to fly. He gave sight to the blind, healed the sick, and fed the hungry.

The Gospels are full of stories of healings at his hands. We see healings of the man born blind, the paralytic, and Peter's mother-in-law, who had been confined to bed with a fever (see Mark 1:30–31). We also have the stories of the miraculous feeding of the multitudes (Mark 6:30–44; 8:1–8). If this is how Jesus used his divine power, we too should use what power we have to serve the needy.

Jesus also showed charity in his advocacy for the poor. He encouraged the rich man to sell his possessions and give the money to those in need, and he taught the importance of giving alms (see Mark 10:17–22; Luke 6:38). But he emphasized more than giving money as concerned bystanders. Jesus commanded that we meet the physical needs of the poor ourselves. He taught that when we personally minister to the sick, the hungry, and the poor, we are actually showing our love for *him*:

> Then the King will say to those at his right hand, "Come, O blessed of my Father, inherit the kingdom prepared for you from the foundation of the world; for I was hungry and you gave me food, I was thirsty and you gave me drink, I was a stranger and you welcomed me, I was naked and you clothed me, I was sick and you visited me, I was in prison and you came to me." Then the righteous will answer him, "Lord, when did we see you hungry and feed you, or thirsty and give you drink? And when did we see you a stranger and

welcome you, or naked and clothe you? And when did we see you sick or in prison and visit you?" And the King will answer them, "Truly, I say to you, as you did it to one of the least of these my brethren, you did it to me." (Matthew 25:34–40)

These practical expressions of charity enable us to demonstrate our love for God. As it says in the first letter of St. John, "He who does not love his brother whom he has seen, cannot love God whom he has not seen" (1 John 4:20).

This love is more than an emotion or a sentiment. Jesus expects us to provide for others' physical needs, even to the extent of inviting them to share our table. When he was dining at the home of a Pharisee, he told his host:

When you give a dinner or a banquet, do not invite your friends or your brothers or your kinsmen or rich neighbors, lest they also invite you in return, and you be repaid. But when you give a feast, invite the poor, the maimed, the lame, the blind, and you will be blessed, because they cannot repay you. (Luke 14:12–14)

Jesus calls us to extend charity to others not because of what we will receive in return but because it is part of sharing in his love for us. We are to follow his example of selfless love in the way we care for our neighbors. "A new commandment I give to you, that you love one another; even as I have loved you, that you also love one another" (John 13:34). This basic command appears three times in John's Gospel, along with a description of the telltale sign of Christianity: "By this all men will know that you are my disciples, if you have love for one another" (John 13:35).

This love for others is a visible witness to the world. It is tangible, alive, and active. And we are to love everyone, not just those whom we are naturally inclined to love. Jesus told us we should even love our enemies (see Matthew 5:44; Luke 6:27).

This brings us to another major way Jesus showed charity: by caring for the downtrodden. While others relegated outcasts to the fringes of society, Jesus embraced and ministered to them. He recognized their dignity and shattered the social stigmas that made them untouchable. He regularly broke proscriptions about engaging with sinners and lepers. He associated with tax collectors, ministered to prostitutes, talked with Samaritans, and touched people who were "unclean."

In a society where physical disabilities were seen as a kind of divine stamp of disapproval, Jesus did not hesitate to touch and heal the blind, the lame, and the deaf. In a religious milieu in which women had no authority, Jesus invited them to be his disciples and to join in the work of evangelization. Indeed, he specifically announced that he was sent to "set at liberty those who are oppressed" (Luke 4:18).

Underlying all of his encounters with the downtrodden was Christ's recognition of their human dignity. He did not love people based on their talents, power, or quality of life. He loved people because they were human beings made in the image of God. No one was an anonymous number, nor were their needs frustrating burdens.

Jesus repeatedly reminded his followers of the command "Love your neighbor as yourself" (Matthew 19:19; 22:39; Mark 12:31). Obeying this instruction means recognizing that others, regardless of their abilities or social status, deserve our respect at the very least and often our attention and assistance as well. We cannot treat them as less than ourselves.

And we cannot be selective about who qualifies as our neighbor. As Jesus indicated in the parable of the Good Samaritan, our neighbor is anyone who needs our help (see Luke 10:30–37).

The apostle James encourages us to "be doers of the word, and not hearers only, deceiving yourselves" (James 1:22). He exhorts us specifically in the area of charity:

> What does it profit, my brethren, if a man says he has faith but has not works? Can his faith save him? If a brother or sister is poorly clothed and in lack of daily food, and one of you says to them, "Go in peace, be warmed and filled," without giving them the things needed for the body, what does it profit? So faith by itself, if it has no works, is dead. (James 2:14–17)

As we will see, the Francises have each made a priority of being charitable to others, living out this concrete love in action that is essential to being Christian.

St. Francis and the Needy

St. Francis was never a stingy man. He had a natural liberality about him that led to frequent acts of generosity. Even before he made the firm resolution to conform himself to Christ, he loved to provide for others. Although it was usually out of his father's pocket, the young Francis freely spent money on the amusement of his friends, regularly buying them dinner during their evenings out. But his desire to take care of others' needs extended beyond his own cohorts.

Francis was completing a sale in his father's shop one afternoon when a poor beggar approached him asking for alms. Unsure how to handle the awkward situation, Francis chose to complete the business transaction, and the uninvited mendicant finally gave up and slipped away. As soon as the sale was done, however, Francis felt a pang of remorse. He dropped everything and sprang out of the shop, leaving his father's goods unattended. He ran through the streets until he found the unfortunate fellow and filled the man's pockets with money. The future saint swore to himself that he would never again refuse a poor person in need. His devotion to selfless charity for the needy had awakened.

The haste with which Francis amended his failure in charity and the grand resolution that followed upon it demonstrate his belief that caring for the needs of others is a fundamental human responsibility. Even when it meant making a personal sacrifice, Francis was quick to extend charity to his neighbors. Such an occasion occurred during the phase when Francis was determined to be a knight.

It was Francis's desire to become the groom of an Assisi nobleman who was off to the wars. The young knight aspirant made himself the envy of the local military community by outfitting himself with a fine horse, weapons, and an elegant uniform. Francis felt himself perfectly suited for the task and proudly prepared for departure to the field of battle.

Amid the heat of his excitement, Francis came upon a poor fellow citizen who was unable to participate in the military effort for lack of armor. Francis immediately stripped himself of his own accouterments and gave them freely to the man.

Later, when Francis decided to live his life of absolute poverty, he made a clear distinction between this voluntary poverty for the sake of the Gospel and the sufferings of the poor. Although he went to great lengths to free himself and his friars of material things, Francis's commitment to providing necessities for others was uncompromising.

After the order was well established, for example, Francis directed a young man seeking entrance into the brotherhood, "If you wish to join the Poor of God first give your possessions to the poor of the world."[47] The man dutifully departed and disposed of all of his goods, but he gave everything to his relatives and nothing to the poor. He returned to Francis and described how he had completed this first assignment. "Begone, Friar Fly," Francis said, "because you have not yet emerged from your house and your kinfolk. You have given your possessions to your kinsmen and cheated the poor."[48]

This may have been a harsh lesson for the young man, his future plans now undone and himself destitute as well. But Francis was adamant about the importance of caring for the poor.

Perhaps Francis's love for those in need was best exemplified by the way he cared for his brothers when they were sick and suffering. Upon his return from a trip to Rome in 1210, Francis and his small band of followers took up residence in an abandoned hut not far from the Portiuncula. Here the severe demands of prayer and penance sometimes took their toll upon the brothers. One night all in the hut were awakened by a desperate cry:

> "I'm dying. I'm dying!" moaned a voice. "Get up, brothers! And make a light!" ordered Francis. He asked who was dying. "Me!" said the voice. "What are you dying of, Brother?" "Of Hunger!" At once the saint had the table set, and so that the dying one should not feel ashamed at eating alone, they all ate with him willingly. Francis profited by this opportunity to enjoin upon them less severe fasting, urging

them not to try to imitate him in this. "For," he explained, "I who am at the head of the brotherhood have duties that the rest do not have. And beside I am so made that I need only a little coarse food to live."[49]

On another occasion, Brother Sylvester was not feeling well, but no one noticed. No one, that is, except for Francis, who was sometimes known to the brothers as *mater carissima*, or "beloved mother" because of his tender concern for all of his sons. And so, rising before dawn, Francis hatched a plan to help Sylvester. Thinking that some fresh grapes would do him a great deal of good, Francis awakened Sylvester and took him to a nearby vineyard for a rejuvenating breakfast.

Francis provided for the care of the brothers in his written directions. In the Rule of 1221, he wrote, "If a friar falls ill, no matter where he is, the others may not leave him, unless someone has been appointed to look after him as they should like to be looked after themselves."[50] He repeated this injunction, so similar to the command to "love your neighbor as yourself," in the Rule of 1223. In the Rule for the Third Order of laypeople, he also provided for the sick:

> Whenever any brother or sister happens to fall ill, the ministers, if the patient let them know of it, shall in person or through others visit the patient once a week, and remind him of penance; and if they find it expedient, they are to supply him from the common fund with what he may need for the body.[51]

POPE FRANCIS AND THE NEEDY

When it comes to caring for those in need, Pope Francis has always practiced what he preaches. This man, who has made a priority of visiting terminal cancer patients, washing and kissing the feet of AIDS victims, and walking shoulder to shoulder with the poor, explained in one of his morning homilies the motivation for what he does: It is a way of loving Christ.

> We find Jesus' wounds in carrying out works of mercy, giving to our body—the body—the soul too, but —I stress— the body of your wounded brother, because he is hungry, because he is thirsty, because he is naked, because he is humiliated, because he is a slave, because he's in jail, because he is in the hospital. Those are the wounds of Jesus today. We need to touch the wounds of Jesus, we must caress the wounds of Jesus, we need to bind the wounds of Jesus with tenderness, we have to kiss the wounds of Jesus, and this literally. Just think of what happened to St. Francis, when he embraced the leper?... His life changed.[52]

(We'll hear more about Francis and the leper in the following section!)

On many other occasions, Pope Francis has spoken eloquently on the meaning and importance of serving the needy. In explaining his act of washing and kissing the feet of cancer patients, he emphasized being Christ-like: "This gesture is an invitation to the heart of every Christian, because we never lose if we imitate Jesus, if we...serve our suffering brothers."[53]

In a homily in 2003, he presented charity to the needy as a choice we either embrace or reject daily. "Every economic, political, social, or religious project," he said, "involves the inclusion or exclusion of the wounded lying on the side of the road. Each day, each of us faces the choice of being a Good Samaritan or an indifferent bystander."[54] His words remind us that we cannot be like Charles Dickens's Mr. Scrooge, who avoided giving alms by asking, "Are there no prisons?... And the Union Workhouses?... Are they still in operation?... It's not my business."[55] Pope Francis counsels that it is our business.

> We should not wait until the social security system, currently ruined by pillaging that has gone on, gets back on its feet; there are countless ways in which we can provide a service to our seniors; in the meantime, all we need is goodwill and some creativity. Similarly, we cannot ignore the specific possibilities to do something to help the children and all those who are sick and suffering. The belief that there are "structural" issues, involving society as a whole and the state itself, in no way exempts us from doing our bit, however small.[56]

In a tweet shortly after his election, Pope Francis wrote, "Christ leads us to go out from ourselves more and more, to give ourselves and to serve others."[57] And that's what Jorge Bergoglio has been doing for years.

One ill-fated night in 2004, a fire broke out in a nightclub in Buenos Aires. One hundred seventy-five people were killed and many more injured. Even before many of the firemen and ambulances arrived, then-Archbishop Bergoglio was there, personally consoling the survivors. He made arrangements for their ongoing pastoral care, and he spoke out about regulatory failures and response failures by authorities.

Pope Francis has done his bit for the sick and suffering. There are many day-to-day examples. In Argentina, he traveled around keeping company with the poor in the shantytowns of Buenos

Aires. He regularly served in soup kitchens and baptized the children of the city's parishes. When he encountered beggars around these areas, he made a practice of speaking with them and helping them in some way. One biographer tells this tale:

> Oscar Justo, 60, begs for bills and coins from a perch next to St. Joseph Parish in Barrio de Flores....
>
> As Cardinal Jorge Mario Bergoglio of Buenos Aires, Pope Francis passed by often, walking from the bus stop or surfacing from a nearby subway station. But he always took time to greet Justo, offer a blessing and provide a few pesos.
>
> 'He always gave me something...sometimes 100 pesos ($20)," said Justo...who lost both legs in a railway accident.[58]

The Holy Father believes that we all have a duty not only to meet immediate needs but also to address the underlying causes of poverty. "A Christian's obligation," he tells us, "is to integrate the most deprived into his community in whatever way possible, but definitely to integrate them."[59] The pope calls upon us to seek practical ways to alleviate the suffering of those in need.

> The first attention we pay to poverty is assistance: "Are you hungry? Here, here is something to eat." But our aid cannot end there. We must build toward human promotion and integration in the community. The poor must not be perpetually marginalized. We cannot accept the underlying idea that "We who are doing well give something to those who are doing badly, but they should stay that way, far away from us." That is not Christian. It is indispensable that we integrate them into our community as soon as possible, through education in technical schools...so that

they may get ahead in life. This concept was dominant at the end of the nineteenth century in the schools created by Don Bosco.... Something similar is being done by the priests in the shantytowns of Buenos Aires. They seek to give kids, with a couple years apprenticeship, the means they need to change their lives, to become electricians, cooks, tailors.[60]

Pope Francis is committed to charity in action; he is not interested in empty talk about being charitable. He told a crowd of two hundred thousand two months after his election:

> Today, and it breaks my heart to say it, finding a homeless person who has died of cold, is not news. Today, the news is scandals, that is news, but the many children who don't have food—that's not news. This is grave. We can't rest easy while things are this way.... We cannot become starched Christians, too polite, who speak of theology calmly over tea.... We have to become courageous Christians and seek out those (who need help most).[61]

Pope Francis demonstrates this kind of courage. He does what he believes is charitable, even when it is unconventional or causes people to raise their eyebrows. His unprecedented detour during World Youth Day is a case in point.

Straying from the official areas of plans and preparations and performances, the pope decided to "seek out" the people who live in the slums of Rio de Janeiro. Even in the dangerous gang-ridden Varginha neighborhood, he shunned the safety of his car and walked among the crowds, greeting the poor in person and drawing worldwide attention to their tragic circumstances.

"Let us always remember this," he said to those gathered and to the world watching, "only when we are able to share do we become truly rich; everything that is shared is multiplied! The measure of the greatness of a society is found in the way it treats those most in need, those who have nothing apart from their poverty!"[62]

The pope made an unusual (and unselfish) request after his election, another example of his courage in reaching out to the poor. Just as when he was installed as a cardinal, Pope Francis asked people to consider the poor instead of traveling to Rome to celebrate with him. Archbishop Emil Paul Tscherrig, apostolic nuncio to Argentina, wrote upon Francis's elevation to pope:

> Holy Father Francis has asked me to transmit to all Bishops, Priests, Religious men and women, and to all people of God his cherished recognition for the prayers and expressions of warmth, affection and charity that he has received. At the same time he would wish that, instead of going to Rome for the beginning of his Pontificate next March 19, you may keep this spiritual closeness that is so much appreciated, accompanying it with some gesture of charity towards the neediest.[63]

ST. FRANCIS AND THE DOWNTRODDEN

In his practice of charity, St. Francis was concerned with more than the material needs of the sick and poor. He was also interested in showing compassion to those who were cast aside, rejected, forgotten, or oppressed. Like the Good Samaritan, Francis attended to people whom other people tended to ignore. As G.K. Chesterton put it, "He seems to have liked everybody, but especially those whom everybody disliked him for liking."[64] In his imitation of Christ, St. Francis recognized the dignity of human beings, made in the image of God. Even when that image was hard to discern, Francis had the eyes to see it.

This spiritual vision took a while to develop, however. In his youth Francis was not especially concerned with loving the supposedly unlovable. The first glimpse we have of his treatment of ostracized lepers, for example, reveals a man who could not tolerate being in their presence. Even the thought of their unfortunate deformities nauseated Francis, to the point that if he saw a leper in the distance, he would turn his horse around and avoid the encounter. In this way he aligned himself with a society that declared these men and women to be legally dead.

But one day this all changed. As he rounded the bend in a narrow road, Francis suddenly found himself confronted with a leprous man. Instead of his typical reaction, Francis felt the desire to acknowledge the humanity of this person. He came down off his horse, walked up to the alienated man, embraced him, and gave him alms. The grace of God had filled Francis's heart with charity for this suffering outcast.

Now brimming with sweetness instead of disgust, Francis hopped back on his steed and rode off to visit an entire commune of lepers. Lingering among these ill-fated brethren, cast aside and abandoned as they were, Francis begged their forgiveness for his previous demeaning treatment and proceeded to distribute money to assist them. Then he kissed them all and departed.

A new clarity of vision had come to Francis when he embraced that leper. He conquered the fear and prejudice that previously prevented him from extending charity to this group of people.

And he was never again a slave to discrimination. Instead he developed a habit of acknowledging the dignity of every human person, regardless of circumstances or social status.

Another example of his solidarity with those whom society rejected came when Francis made a trip to the tomb of St. Peter. After leaving his purse of gold coins as an offering at the tomb, Francis had no alms to share with the homeless beggars who occupied the area outside. Rather than sneaking past and pretending not to notice them, Francis decided to join them. He exchanged his handsome clothes for the shabby rags of one destitute man, begged along with the motley group, and shared a humble meal with them.

These unconventional expressions of charity were indicators of Francis's courage, both physical and social. Because he overcame his fears, he was free to extend charity to all. Never a conformist, Francis plowed ahead on the path he thought right, regardless of the harsh judgment of those around him. He ministered to the downtrodden without concern for any personal repercussions.

This attitude extended to women. In Francis's time a woman was hardly an equal member of society. She generally could not work outside of the domestic sphere, could not receive a formal education, and could not decide for herself whether or not to marry or even whom her husband was to be. To put it simply, her options were limited.

Francis was no slave to societal expectations. He followed the example of Jesus, who always upheld the dignity of women and broke the fossilized norms that stifled their freedom. So it was that when Clare, a beautiful young woman from a wealthy family in Assisi, came to Francis for help, he didn't send her back to her father but instead listened to her plea. Clare wanted the life of poverty and simplicity that Francis had chosen. She wished to be the bride of Christ instead of the wife of a nobleman of her father's choosing.

Francis discerned Clare's sincerity and went on, for a full year, to serve as her spiritual mentor and guide. Clare's family disapproved of this friendship, but she completed her novitiate nonetheless. Then, in a sort of spiritual elopement, Clare fled her home in the dark of night to take her religious vows at the Portiuncula. There, honoring the wishes of this brave woman, Francis cut off her long blonde tresses and replaced them with a veil. Clare vowed to follow Jesus in poverty according to the rule of her teacher, Francis.

Soon other women came to Francis hoping to enjoy the same freedom he had made possible for Clare. He treated them all with dignity, respecting their wishes instead of patting them on the head and sending them back home. He received the promises of Clare's sister, Agnes, even in the face of armed opposition from her family.

Thanks to Francis's assistance, the order of Poor Clares came to be, and it grew in tandem with the Friars Minor. Francis maintained a close and respectful relationship with the new women's order for the rest of his life. Never relegating the women to second-class status, he showed the same charity for them that he showed his brothers. He wrote to Clare: "I desire and promise you personally and in the name of my friars that I will always have the same loving care and special solicitude for you as for them."[65]

Pope Francis and the Downtrodden

Whether he is giving a speech, delivering a homily, composing a letter, or writing a book, Pope Francis rarely neglects an opportunity to speak about the dignity of the human person. He consistently points out the importance of treating everyone with respect, recognizing their infinite worth as children of God. He has shown himself a champion not only for the poor and sick but for all those who are marginalized by society in any way. The unborn, the elderly, women, victims of child abuse and human trafficking, migrants, the lonely, the forgotten, children of unwed mothers, those who suffer because of sin, and those who just don't fit in for any reason—these have all been the beneficiaries of his passionate pleas for kindness, concern, and benevolence. Clearly the pope's heart is filled with a true and special compassion for "the least of these" (Matthew 25:40).

In their faces the Holy Father sees Christ.

> In the fragile human being each one of us is invited to recognize the face of the Lord, who in his human flesh experienced the indifference and solitude to which we often condemn the poorest, whether in developing countries or in wealthy societies. Every unborn child, though unjustly condemned to be aborted, has the face of the Lord, who even before his birth, and then as soon as he was born, experienced the rejection of the world. And every old person, even if infirm and at the end of his days, carries with him the face of Christ. They must not be thrown away![66]

In a message from the Vatican to Catholics in Ireland, Scotland, England, and Wales, on the occasion of their Day for Life, we have a summary of Francis's ideals:

Calling to mind the teaching of Saint Irenaeus that the glory of God is seen in a living human being, the Holy Father encourages all of you to let the light of that glory shine so brightly that everyone may come to recognize the inestimable value of all human life. Even the weakest and most vulnerable, the sick, the old, the unborn and the poor, are masterpieces of God's creation, made in his own image, destined to live forever, and deserving of the utmost reverence and respect.[67]

Pope Francis has put his power at the service of the downtrodden and has asked other leaders to do the same. In a letter to David Cameron, British prime minister, on the occasion of the G8 meeting in June 2013, Pope Francis wrote:

The goal of economics and politics is to serve humanity, beginning with the poorest and most vulnerable wherever they may be, even in their mothers' wombs. Every economic and political theory or action must set about providing each inhabitant of the planet with the minimum wherewithal to live in dignity and freedom, with the possibility of supporting a family, educating children, praising God and developing one's own human potential. This is the main thing; in the absence of such a vision, all economic activity is meaningless.[68]

The Holy Father also speaks out against the abuse of power that wounds the vunerable. In reference to the clergy abuse scandal he said:

You cannot be in a position of power and destroy the life of another person.... A bishop once called me to ask me by phone what to do in a situation like that, and I told him to take away the priests' licenses, not to allow them to exercise the priesthood any more, and to begin a canonical trial in that diocese's court.[69]

Francis has spoken out on behalf of the homeless, particularly the young. In a homily while still archbishop, he noted:

> There are kids who've lived in the streets for years...and the city failed and continues to fail in any attempt to free them from this structural slavery of homelessness....
>
> Girls are kidnapped and subjected to use and abuse of their body; they are destroyed in their dignity. The human flesh that Jesus assumed and for which he died is worth less than the flesh of a house pet. We take better care of a dog than these slaves who we kick, who we destroy.[70]

The pope speaks out for the old as well. In his book *On Heaven and Earth* he writes:

> Parents work and they have to resort to a nursing home to take care of the grandparents, but many times it is not an issue of being busy at work, but mere egoism: the elderly are bothersome in the house, they smell bad.... There are families in which there is no other option.... But in many cases, when I visit nursing homes, I ask the elderly about their children and they answer that they have to work: they try to cover for them. There are many who abandon those who fed them, educated them, wiped their bottoms. It hurts me; it makes me weep inside. We will not speak of what I call covert euthanasia; the poor attention to the elderly in

hospitals and in health insurance that does not give them the medicine and attention they need.[71]

He has also spoken about the dignity of women and the need to ensure a place for the feminine perspective in ecclesiastical decision making. Without suggesting a change in the doctrine of the priesthood, he nonetheless advocates the essential role of women in the Church: "The church cannot be herself without the woman and her role. The woman is essential for the church.... The feminine genius is needed wherever we make important decisions."[72]

Pope Francis speaks with compassion for single mothers. In 2012 he preached against religious hypocrisy toward them:

> In our ecclesiastical region there are priests who don't baptize children of single mothers because they weren't conceived in the sanctity of marriage. These are today's hypocrites. Those who clericalize the Church. Those who separate the people of God from salvation. And this poor girl who, rather than returning the child to sender, had the courage to carry it into the world, must wander from parish to parish so that it's baptized.[73]

His concern extends to prostitutes. He courageously declared in a homily in Buenos Aires:

> In this city there are many slaves!... The night before last a poor girl was taken out of a brothel and had to be hospitalized in intensive care at one of our hospitals because to break her will they gave her psychotropics, and she entered a coma.... That happens in this city! This city makes these great mafia lords very elegant! They may eat in Puerto Madero

restaurants, but their money is stained with blood.... They are enslavers![74]

There are two curious and important things to be aware of in order to fully understand Pope Francis's teachings on charity. The first is his belief that charity must be without vanity. In his book with Rabbi Abraham Skorka, the future pope relates the story of a benefit dinner attended by the cream of the crop at which a gold Rolex watch was auctioned off to raise money for the poor.

> What a disgrace; how humiliating. That was a bad use of charity. It sought a person who would use this watch for vanity in order to feed the poor.... Sometimes things are done in the name of charity that are not charitable; they are like crude caricatures of a good intention. There is no charity without love, and if vanity is a part of helping the needy, there is no love; it is feigned charity.[75]

The second element to be aware of is Pope Francis's insistence that charity must be personal. He tells us that in Christianity our charity should include human contact:

> This commitment must be person to person, in the flesh. It is not enough to mediate this commitment through institutions, which obviously help because they have a multiplying effect, but that is not enough. They do not excuse us from our obligation of establishing personal contact with the needy. The sick must be cared for, even when we find them repulsive and repugnant. Those in prison must be visited.[76]

When hearing confessions, Francis sometimes asks penitents if they give alms to beggars. He continues, "Do you look them in the eyes? Do you touch their hand?"[77]

It is not enough to throw someone a coin and look the other way. We must be willing to touch our neighbor, the pope tells us. True charity must be both personal and without vanity. In this way it imparts dignity to both the giver and the receiver.

FOR REFLECTION: HOW WILL I RESPOND?

Catechism of the Catholic Church 1823: "Jesus makes charity the new commandment. By loving his own 'to the end,' he makes manifest the Father's love which he receives. By loving one another, the disciples imitate the love of Jesus which they themselves receive. Whence Jesus says: 'As the Father has loved me, so have I loved you; abide in my love.' And again: 'This is my commandment, that you love one another as I have loved you.'"

Consider: How would I describe Christ's love for me? When have I succeeded at loving my family and friends this way? When have I struggled to do so? What spiritual resolution(s) would help me to "abide" in the love of Christ?

● ● ●

Pope Francis takes the Gospel to the street. He does not wait for those in need to approach him; he goes to them, visiting the poor and sick in a spirit of true charity. And as he tells us, we have to become "courageous Christians" in order to do this.

Consider: How courageous am I when it comes to serving the needy? Are there fears that prevent me from reaching out to the poor or the sick as much as I should? If so, what are the root causes of these fears? How can I strive to overcome them?

● ● ●

St. Francis did not draw lines between himself and society's outcasts. He stepped into their shoes, at times quite literally. This both enabled him to help and enabled people to trust him. Even when it jeopardized his own social status, he showed respect and love for the downtrodden.

Consider: Am I willing to associate myself with those on the fringes of society? What have I done to assist the imprisoned, the homeless, the elderly, the unborn? Whom do I know that is downtrodden? How can I show respect for his or her dignity as a human being?

CHAPTER THREE
The Church

We must also fast and abstain from vices and sins and from any excess of food and drink, and be Catholics.[78]

—St. Francis

The Church is not a charitable, cultural or political association, but a living Body, that walks and acts in history. And this Body has a head, Jesus, who guides, nourishes and supports it.[79]

—Pope Francis

A saint and a pope—it doesn't get much more Catholic than that. There is a kind of symbiotic relationship between the two: The one boasts a formal stamp of approval from the Catholic Church recognizing the holiness to which all Christians are called; the other has the power to give out the stamps. Both strive to make the Church an effective instrument of Christ's work on earth.

And in a certain sense, each stands as a symbol of a particular aspect of the Church's identity. The saint symbolizes the community of believers, the people of God, as the Second Vatican Council described the Church. And the pope symbolizes the institutional, hierarchical element of the Church, which exists to teach, shepherd, and sanctify the people of God.

The union of these two aspects of the Church—communal and institutional—is a mysterious one. We refer to the Church itself as "the Mystical Body of Christ," emphasizing that we, the believers, are the body, and Christ is the head. Love for Christ necessarily includes love of his body. And so it is that the Francises, because they love Christ, also love the Church.

The Gospel testimony about the Church emphasizes its intimate connection to the will of Christ. In a pivotal exchange with the disciples, Jesus asks the probing question, "But who do you say that I am?" (Matthew 16:15). Simon (Peter) is the one who responds with faith: "You are the Christ, the Son of the living God" (Matthew 16:16). In response Jesus announces that Simon is blessed because God revealed this truth to him.

And now comes the climactic moment when Jesus gives Simon a new identity and appoints him with a new mission: "And I tell you, you are Peter, and on this rock I will build *my* Church, and the gates of Hades shall not prevail against it" (Matthew 16:18, emphasis added).

Here, Jesus has announced his intentions. He is planning to build a church, *his* Church. This is not Peter's plan; it's Christ's plan. He intends to establish a thing that can be built, and that means it has a structure. It's not just an idea; it is in fact an institution.

Furthermore, he is planning to build this thing on the foundation of human cooperation. This institution is intimately connected to the faith of the people, as articulated by the declaration of Simon, now *Petros*, Peter, Rock. Thus we already see Christ's will that the Church be both an institution (with a hierarchy established through the primacy of Peter) and an expression of the faith of believers (symbolized by Peter's own faith).

The early Christians understood the Church's identity as being twofold in this way. Hence we have various scriptural references to the leadership of bishops and deacons (see Philippians 1:1; 1 Timothy 3:1–13; Titus 1:7) along with the authority of the institutional Church (see Acts 15:1–6). And we also see numerous scriptural references to the Church as the active community of believers, the body of Christ.

St. Paul, for example, in his first letter to the Corinthians, describes how the believers, in all their diversity, constitute the Church: "Now you are the body of Christ and individually members of it. And God has appointed in the Church first apostles, second prophets, third teachers, then workers of miracles, then healers, helpers, administrators, speakers in various kinds of tongues" (1 Corinthians 12:27–28). He makes a similar point in his letter to the Romans: "For as in one body we have many members, and all the members do not have the same function, so we, though many, are one body in Christ, and individually members one of another" (Romans 12:4–5).

Paul also clarifies that Christ is always the head of the body. Christ has the ultimate authority, which works through the Church that he instituted. In his Letter to the Colossians, Paul says simply: "He is the head of the body, the Church" (Colossians 1:18). Paul also expresses this idea in the book of Ephesians: "[God] has put all things under his feet and has made him the head over all things for the Church, which is his body" (Ephesians 1:22–23). Later in the same epistle, Paul emphasizes the love that Christ has for the Church: "For no man ever hates his own flesh, but nourishes and cherishes it, as Christ does the Church, because we are members of his body" (Ephesians 5:29–30).

This love, of course, culminated in the sacrifice that Christ made on the cross. There he laid down his life for the sake of the community of believers. Paul writes, "Christ loved the Church and gave himself up for her, that he might sanctify her" (Ephesians

5:25–26). In the Acts of the Apostles, we hear Paul remind the leaders of the Church that their role in the hierarchy is a sharing in the sacrificial love of Christ: "Take heed to yourselves and to all the flock, in which the Holy Spirit has made you guardians, to feed the Church of the Lord which he obtained with his own blood" (Acts 20:28).

The connection between Christ's sacrifice on the cross and his body the Church is perhaps most mysteriously evident in the gift of the Eucharist, the Body and Blood of Christ. As Jesus emphasized at the Last Supper, this sacrament links the physical offering of his Body with the salvation of the faithful. Believers receive this sacrament as members of the Church, and it in turn strengthens them to become more fervent members of the body.

Indeed, the sacrament of the Eucharist, and all the other sacraments, reveal in themselves the twofold nature of the Church. Without the institution that continues administering the sacraments, the members of the body could not receive them at all. And it is precisely through the sacraments, particularly the Eucharist, that the unity of the body of Christ is assured. As Paul writes, "The cup of blessing which we bless, is it not a participation in the blood of Christ? The bread which we break, is it not a participation in the body of Christ? Because there is one bread, we who are many are one body, for we all partake of the one bread" (1 Corinthians 10:16–17).

Catholics understand their relationship to Christ, and the very practice of their faith, in connection with the Church. Thus, trying to understand the spirituality of either St. Francis or Pope Francis apart from the Church simply wouldn't make sense. The faith of both men was born and nurtured within the embrace of "holy mother the hierarchical church,"[80] as Pope Francis has called it, and both men chose to dedicate their entire lives to serving the Church in return. Each of them respects the authority of the hierarchical Church, and each of them demonstrates a love for Christ's body, the Church. Indeed, because Christ loves the Church, they do too.

ST. FRANCIS AND CHURCH AUTHORITY

Many different people love St. Francis for many different reasons. Some appreciate his love of nature, others admire his commitment to poverty, and still others gravitate toward him because of his advocacy for peace. But as we have seen, whatever cause he championed was really the *effect* of his love for Christ and his desire to imitate the Lord. He was not political; he was evangelical. He lived, loved, served, and preached the Gospel.

Francis's activity as a Church reformer was no exception. He did help reform the Church, but not as one who was angry or disgruntled. Francis reformed the Church as a good wife reforms her husband or a good husband reforms his wife: out of love. Because St. Francis loved Christ, he naturally loved the bride of Christ as well.

Francis's unwavering adherence to Church teaching and his respectful obedience to Church leadership reveal his faithfulness to the hierarchy that Jesus established. In fact, Francis found the authority of the Church to be a source of confidence as he charted his unprecedented course in religious life. The way to be sure he was authentically following Christ was to seek the guidance and approval of Christ's Church.

So it was that in the spring of the year 1210, when his band of brothers was in its infancy, he and eleven of his followers traveled to Rome. Their reason for the journey was to seek the sanction of Pope Innocent III. Francis hoped to receive permission and a blessing to live the life of poverty to which he felt called.

There is no shortage of stories about this meeting with the pope. Was Francis, in his tattered garments, really mistaken for a swineherd by the Holy Father? Is it true that His Holiness told Francis to return to his pigs and preach all the sermons he wanted to them? Did Francis in fact depart immediately, find the nearest pigsty, smear himself in the muck, and return to Innocent declaring, "My lord, now that I have done what you commanded, please be good enough to grant me my request"?[81]

And what of Innocent's dream? Did the pope in fact recognize Francis, upon his return, as the little religious who in the dream lent his shoulder to support the toppling Lateran Basilica? Or perhaps the pontiff was persuaded by the advice of Cardinal Giovanni of San Paolo, "If we reject the petition of this poor man with the excuse that the Rule is new and too austere when he petitions us to approve a form of life that is in keeping with the Gospel, we must fear that we may displease the very Gospel of Christ."[82]

Regardless of the details, it is clear that Francis earnestly desired the approval of the pope, that he sought it, and that he did eventually receive it. Indeed, Francis so trusted the authority of the Church that he could only be content once the Holy Father gave his assurance that Francis's way of life was a legitimate means of following the Gospel.

Francis sought the blessing of the Church in other ways as well. When his friars traveled to preach, for example, Francis insisted that they do so only with the permission of the local priest or bishop. The reputation of the brothers was such that permission was typically granted. But on one occasion the bishop of Imola denied Francis his request to preach, informing him, "I am here for that purpose and I don't need anyone to tell me what to do."[83]

Now Francis had the opportunity to demonstrate his respect, and this he did by bowing politely and departing. The saint was obedient, but he was also persistent. He returned an hour later to the surprise of the bishop. "Are you back again? What do you want now?"

"Your Excellency," Francis replied, "when a father drives his son out the door, there is nothing left for him to do but to come back in through the window. So I, as your loving son, have not hesitated to come back to see you."

The bishop, moved by Francis's courtesy, charm, and respectfulness, instantly embraced him and granted all the friars permission to preach in his diocese whenever they wished.[84]

Francis shaped his religious order in harmony with his desire to be obedient to Church authority. He prescribed that the ministers of the order "ask of the Lord Pope one of the Cardinals of the holy Roman Church to be governor, protector, and corrector of this brotherhood, so that being always subject and submissive at the feet of the same holy Church, grounded in the Catholic faith, we may observe poverty and humility and the holy Gospel of our Lord Jesus Christ, which we have firmly promised."[85]

Francis wrote in his First Rule, "No candidate may be received contrary to the norms and prescriptions of the Church."[86] Later in the same document, he instructed, "No friar may preach contrary to Church law."[87] And he added, "All the friars are bound to be Catholics, and live and speak as such. Anyone who abandons the

Catholic faith or practice by word or deed must be absolutely excluded from the Order, unless he repents."[88]

Until his dying day, Francis's devotion to the Church, to her priests, and to the Eucharist, which she alone can provide, never waned. When his health was deteriorating, the brothers asked him to give a written testimony of his last wishes. In it, he wrote that the brothers "must ever humbly and faithfully obey the prelates and clergy of our holy Mother the Church."[89]

He encouraged the laity to show this respect as well, in his Letter to All the Faithful: "We ought, moreover, to be good Catholics, to visit churches and to confess our sins to the priests, who though sinners themselves, are nonetheless God's ministers and deserving of our respect." On his deathbed, in his final testament, Francis explained the reason why he believed this respect was due to priests:

> The Lord gave me, and gives me now, towards priests who live according to the law of the Holy Roman Church, so great a confidence by reason of their priesthood, and even if they sought to persecute me, I would nonetheless return to them. And if I were to have as great a wisdom as Solomon possessed, and were to meet with poor priests of this world, I do not wish to preach without their consent in the parishes in which they dwell. And these and all others I desire to reverence as my lords.... And for this reason I do this: because in this world I see nothing with my bodily eyes of Him who is the most high Son of God except His most holy Body and His most [holy] Blood, which they receive and which they alone minister to others.[90]

Clearly Francis understood the connection between the authority of the hierarchical Church and the gift of the sacraments. But he was no blind idealist. He knew that the grace of God in the sacraments worked in spite of sinful ministers. There were corrupt members of the Church then, as there are now and as there have always been, and Francis knew it. But he understood well the spiritual power of the Church that Christ instituted, against which "the gates of Hades shall not prevail" (Matthew 16:18).

This humble submission to the Church was, for Francis, really a submission to Christ. Loving the Church was the natural effect of his complete commitment to the Gospel.

POPE FRANCIS AND CHURCH AUTHORITY

Some people have the mistaken impression that being pope is like being God, at least in terms of issuing moral decrees and determining Church doctrine. But it's not so. The pope cannot enshrine his personal ideologies as Church teaching and call them dogma. The successor of St. Peter gets his authority from the same place St. Peter got it: Christ. The pope is subservient to the teachings of Christ that have been passed down and preserved in the heart of the Church.

Thus our Holy Father Francis knows he is subject to the authority of the Church. What the Church teaches, Francis teaches. Consider the following interview with a member of the press during his return flight from World Youth Day in Rio de Janeiro:

> *Patricia Zorzan*: Society has changed, young people have changed, and in Brazil we have seen a great many young people. You did not speak about abortion, about same-sex marriage. In Brazil a law has been approved which widens

the right to abortion and permits marriage between people of the same sex. Why did you not speak about this?

Pope Francis: The Church has already spoken quite clearly on this. It was unnecessary to return to it, just as I didn't speak about cheating, lying, or other matters on which the Church has a clear teaching!

Patricia Zorzan: But the young are interested in this…

Pope Francis: Yes, though it wasn't necessary to speak of it, but rather of the positive things that open up the path to young people. Isn't that right! Besides, young people know perfectly well what the Church's position is.

Patricia Zorzan: What is Your Holiness's position, if we may ask?

Pope Francis: The position of the Church. I am a son of the Church.[91]

Pope Francis describes his role as supreme pontiff with this striking image of love and loyalty: He is a son of the Church. "Mother Church" is a traditional title for Christ's body on earth, after all. And Pope Francis believes in the goodness of this maternal influence. "The Church is Mother," he once said, "and talks to the people as a mother talks to her child, with that confidence that the child already knows that everything he is being taught is for his good, because he knows he is loved."[92]

This helps to clarify Pope Francis's respect for the authority of the Church. What the Church teaches, even in regard to the hot-button issues of the day—abortion, euthanasia, homosexual marriage, withholding Communion from Catholics who publicly oppose Church teaching, divorce, and so on—is for our good. But the Holy Father doesn't harp on these issues because the teaching of the Church is clear and well known. Instead of focusing on what's forbidden, Francis chooses to speak on what Christianity offers. His approach is more pastoral than authoritative.

For those who wonder why they have seen a change of tone in the papacy but no change in teachings, Francis explains that the pope's position is the position of the Church. The Church is an institution that believes itself authorized and capable of teaching truth. And Pope Francis lovingly and consistently upholds this truth.

Thus he has spoken with passion in support of the Church's positions on many controversial topics. As archbishop of Buenos Aires, he opposed the legalization of abortion, accusing the government of failing to respect the majority view of Argentinians and of trying to cause the Church "to waver in our defense of the dignity of the person."[93] He noted:

> A pregnant woman isn't carrying a toothbrush in her stomach, or a tumor. Science has taught us that from the moment of conception, the new being has its entire genetic code. It's impressive. [94]

Speaking on the sanctity of life in general, he declared, "To protect life from its beginning to its end, how simple a thing, how beautiful."[95] In 2007 he presented the final version of a joint statement of the bishops of Latin America known as the Aparecida Document. It states in part,

> We hope that legislators, heads of government, and health professionals, conscious of the dignity of human life and of the rootedness of the family in our peoples, will defend and protect it from the abominable crimes of abortion and euthanasia; that is their responsibility. [96]

The same statement speaks clearly about the Church's teaching on reception of Communion.

We should commit ourselves to "eucharistic coherence," the document says, "that is, we should be conscious that people cannot receive Holy Communion and at the same time act or speak against the commandments, in particular when abortion, euthanasia, and other grave crimes against life and family are facilitated. This responsibility applies particularly to legislators, governors, and health professionals."[97]

The Holy Father has also defended Church prohibitions against the reception of Communion by those divorced and remarried without a declaration of nullity. And in 2010 he led the fight to protest legalization of same-sex marriage in Argentina, saying it was neither a political struggle nor a legislative project "but rather a 'move' of the father of lies who wishes to confuse and deceive the children of God."[98]

However, instead of making a point of judging and condemning those who violate the Church's often challenging moral teachings, Pope Francis chooses to emphasize God's mercy and forgiveness. "The thing the Church needs most today," he said in an interview several months after becoming pope, "is the ability to heal wounds and to warm the hearts of the faithful."[99] Without minimizing the gravity of sin, he wants to show those who feel distanced from the Church a way back into the fold. In his second homily as pope, at St. Anna Parish in the Vatican, Pope Francis preached:

Jesus has this message for us: mercy. I think—and I say it with humility—that this is the Lord's most powerful message: mercy....

It is not easy to entrust oneself to God's mercy, because it is an abyss beyond our comprehension. But we must! "Oh, Father, if you knew my life, you would not say that to me!" "Why, what have you done?" "Oh, I am a great sinner!" "All the better! Go to Jesus: he likes you to tell him these things!" He forgets, he has a very special capacity for forgetting. He forgets, he kisses you, he embraces you and he simply says to you: "Neither do I condemn you; go, and sin no more" (John 8:11). That is the only advice he gives you. After a month, if we are in the same situation…. Let us go back to the Lord. The Lord never tires of forgiving: never! It is we who tire of asking his forgiveness. Let us ask for the grace not to tire of asking forgiveness, because he never tires of forgiving. Let us ask for this grace.[100]

God's limitless forgiveness, however, is never an excuse to persist in our sin. Pope Francis preaches in the spirit of Christ: "The Lord's mercy motivates us to do better."[101]

This approach of loyalty to the Church alongside pastoral compassion for those who struggle with Church teaching is becoming a trademark of Francis's pontificate. Perhaps it is through this balanced approach that the Holy Father hopes to bridge the unfortunate gap between so-called liberal and conservative Catholics. Helping to heal such divisions and bringing greater unity between these factions would be a great service to the Church that Francis loves.

Arriving at this kind of harmony requires a proper understanding of the nature and mission of the Church. The Church is not merely a human institution; it is a divine institution that God has entrusted to the care of humans. Francis is trying to communicate an understanding of the Church as led by the Holy Spirit and centered on Christ.

For example, on the second full day of his pontificate, Pope Francis held an audience for the army of media members who were in Rome for the conclave, many of whom were not Catholic. He asked them to "try to understand more fully the true nature of the Church, as well as her journey in this world, with her virtues and her sins, and to know the spiritual concerns which guide her and are the most genuine way to understand her." He explained:

> The Church is certainly a human and historical institution with all that that entails, yet her nature is not essentially political but spiritual: the Church is the People of God, the Holy People of God making its way to encounter Jesus Christ. Only from this perspective can a satisfactory account be given of the Church's life and activity.... As Benedict XVI frequently reminded us, Christ is present in the Church and guides her.[102]

He also presented this idea in his homily to the cardinal electors: "We can walk as much as we want, we can build many things, but if we do not profess Jesus Christ, things go wrong. We may become a charitable NGO, but not the Church, the Bride of the Lord."[103]

Clearly, Pope Francis understands the Church to be intimately connected to Christ and Christ's work on earth. Perhaps his perspective is best encapsulated by what he said during a catechesis at the International Eucharistic Congress in 2008: "By defending her identity and infallibility, the Church defends the conduit through which the gift of life to the world passes."[104]

This exalted vision of Church authority is not blind obedience to a set of arbitrary teachings. For Pope Francis the Church's infallibility serves the greater purpose of illuminating the truth that brings the fullness of life to the world.

St. Francis and the Body of Christ

In a special revelation, God asked St. Francis to rebuild the Church. The story is one of the most famous in the annals of Franciscan lore. As St. Bonaventure tells it:

> One day when Francis went out to meditate in the fields he was passing by the church of San Damiano which was threatening to collapse because of extreme age. Inspired by the Spirit, he went inside to pray…. While his tear-filled eyes were gazing at the Lord's cross, he heard with his bodily ears a voice coming from the cross, telling him three times: "Francis, go and repair my house which, as you see, is falling into ruin." Trembling with fear, Francis was amazed at the sound of this astonishing voice, since he was alone in the church….
>
> He prepared to put his whole heart into obeying the command he had received. He began zealously to repair the church materially, although the [principal] intention of the words referred to that Church which Christ purchased with his own blood, as the Holy Spirit afterward made him realize.[105]

It took Francis a while, but eventually he understood that God wasn't talking about doing the repairs with mortar and stone. He meant that Francis was called to help resuscitate the vitality of the Mystical Body of Christ.

The members of the Church, at this point in history, were in need of what we might call today a "renewal." In his encyclical on St. Francis, Pope Leo XIII described the situation:

> Licentiousness had greatly impaired popular morality, and nothing was more needed by men than a return to Christian sentiments....
>
> Those even who ought by their profession to have been an example to others had not avoided defiling themselves with the prevalent vices.[106]

Enter Francis Bernardone. As Leo XIII put it, "With wondrous resolution and simplicity he undertook to place before the eyes of the aging world, in his words and deeds, the complete model of Christian perfection."[107]

Through his example and his preaching, Francis reformed the Church. Out of love for Christ and love for Christians, he went from town to town, sometimes visiting as many as five villages in a day, preaching the Gospel from the steps of a building or from atop a bale of straw. But he never climbed up on his soapbox without first practicing what he preached. He was an effective teacher because he was an authentic witness.

Yet Francis did not expect everyone to live the Gospel exactly as he did. He understood that the body of Christ has many members, who are each called to serve God in his or her own way. In spite of his personal commitment to poverty, for example, he never condemned the wealthy for following a different path. With respect and humility, he approached the powerful leaders of the Church to seek their approval of his choice to follow the path of poverty. He counted among his friends such wealthy and powerful men as Cardinal Ugolino (the future Pope Gregory IX) and Count Roland, who gave Francis a beautiful refuge at Mount La Verna late in his life.

Francis understood clearly that the diverse gifts of the body are not to be used in pride and vanity. The Rule of 1221 reads:

> I entreat all my friars, whether they are given to preaching, praying, or manual labor, to do their best to humble themselves at every opportunity; not to boast or be self-satisfied, or take pride in any good which God says or does or accomplishes in them or by them; as our Lord Himself put it, *"Do not rejoice in this, that the spirits are subject to you."* (Luke 10:20)[108]

By offering guidance, even to those with gifts and roles different from his own, Francis sought to build up the body of Christ. He wrote letters to people of a wide range of social and ecclesiastical ranks, advising them according to their own stations. In this way he encouraged many groups to do their part to build up the Church.

In his "Letter to the Rulers of the People," for example, he advises magistrates, consuls, judges, and governors all over the world, "See to it that God is held in great reverence among your subjects; every evening, at a signal given by a herald or in some other way, praise and thanks should be given to the Lord God almighty by all the people."[109] This kind of widespread, public support of Christianity was part of the renewal the Church needed.

Emphasizing mercy was also necessary in order to resuscitate the Church in this period of moral wandering. Thus Francis advised in his "Letter to a Minister," "There should be no friar in the whole world who has fallen into sin, no matter how far he has fallen, who will ever fail to find your forgiveness for the asking, if he will only look into your eyes. And if he does not ask forgiveness, you should ask him if he wants it."[110]

In his "Letter to All the Faithful," Francis spoke of mercy again: "Those who have been entrusted with the power of judging others should pass judgment mercifully, just as they themselves hope to obtain mercy from God."[111] In the same letter, he discussed the compassion that members of the Church should have for one another:

> The man who is in authority and is regarded as the superior should...be as sympathetic with each one of them as he would wish others to be with him.... If one of his brothers falls into sin, he should not be angry with him; on the contrary, he should correct him gently, with all patience and humility, and encourage him.[112]

Another central element of Francis's renewal was reverence for the Eucharist. He was devoted to Christ's Body, Blood, Soul, and Divinity present in the Eucharist. In reminding Christians of the significance of the sacrament, Francis helped solidify the faith of the people. He spoke often about the Blessed Sacrament and the need to reverence it and partake of it. To his brothers he wrote:

> When they have confessed their sins with due contrition, they should receive the Body and Blood of our Lord Jesus Christ with great humility and reverence, remembering the words of our Lord Himself, "*He who eats my flesh and drinks my blood has everlasting Life*" (John 6:55), and "Do this in remembrance of me." (Luke 22:19)[113]

He wished clergy to "tell the people of the need to do penance, impressing on them that no one can be saved unless he receives the Body and Blood of our Lord."[114] And in his "Testament," this man who went to uncommon lengths to deprive himself of the riches of the world insisted, "*Above everything else*, I want the most holy Sacrament to be honored and venerated and reserved in places which are *richly* ornamented."[115] In an era of greed and material excess, Francis recognized the place where true riches lie.

St. Bonaventure records that Francis "burned with love for the Sacrament of our Lord's Body with all his heart, and was lost in wonder at the thought of such condescending love, such loving condescension. He received Holy Communion often and so devoutly that he roused others to devotion too."[116]

This rousing of others was precisely what Francis did so well. He valued and respected everyone, no matter their gifts, and empowered people to use their gifts for the good of the Church. His influence was so positive and so profound that many individuals whom he encountered desired to imitate and follow him. Thus the Franciscan order came to exist, with the Friars Minor for male religious, the Poor Clares for women religious, and eventually the Third Order for laypeople.

As a vibrant community of Christians who shared his charism, the Franciscans in turn contributed to the renewal of the Church in the thirteenth century, as they continue to do today. The contributions of St. Francis to the health and well-being of the Church may, over the course of eight centuries, be without parallel.

Pope Francis and the Body of Christ

No doubt it was a dramatic moment when Cardinal Tarcisio Bertone cut the red ribbon that sealed the papal apartments and gave Pope Francis the key to his new residence. The newly elected pontiff politely entered for a tour of the rooms, but as the world soon found out, this was not destined to be his home. Instead Pope Francis chose to reside in an apartment in Domus Sanctae Marthae. As well as being the residence of the cardinals during the conclave, this is also a guesthouse in Vatican City with a few dozen permanent residents.

Many presumed that this was merely another example of the new pope's penchant for simplicity and poverty. But in response to a question at a news conference, Francis shed further light on the decision:

> You mentioned the fact that I remained at *Santa Marta*. But I could not live alone in the Palace, and it is not luxurious.... I cannot live alone or with just a few people! I need people, I need to meet people, to talk to people. And that's why, when the children from the Jesuit schools asked me: "Why did you do that? For austerity, for poverty?" No, it was for psychological reasons, simply, because psychologically I can't do otherwise.[117]

Some individuals draw energy from having people around them. Pope Francis is one of these. He is a people person. He naturally engages himself with the people he encounters every day and seems to be strengthened by their presence. As he has said, "A thing that is really important for me [is] community. I was always looking for a community. I did not see myself as a priest on my own. I need a community."[118]

This special inclination that God gave him is now equipping him to forge a powerful rapport with people. His way of interacting with his flock is one example of how he hopes to build up the body of Christ. It is a very concrete, very individualized, very personal approach that lets people know they too are valuable, irreplaceable members of the Church.

Examples abound of how the Holy Father has fostered this sense of importance among people from all walks of life. As he put it, "Jesus does not tell the Apostles and us to form an exclusive group, an elite group."[119] Rather, Pope Francis reaches out even to the common people.

On the fourth day of his papacy, for instance, much to the chagrin of his security personnel, he warmly greeted every single person after Mass at a local parish, giving a special embrace to each child he met. What a testimony this was to the Holy Father's appreciation for those who came to church! He then proceeded to walk along the street, greeting and shaking hands with the throngs that waited outside.

When a nine-year-old boy spontaneously ran out of the crowd at World Youth Day in Rio de Janeiro to greet the pope, Francis kindly spoke to him, warmly embraced him, then sent him back to his parents as the young boy wept tears of joy from the priceless encounter. When the pope took possession of St. John Lateran Basilica—the cathedral church of the diocese of Rome—he took a lengthy pause to personally greet a vast lineup of men and women confined to wheelchairs and their caregivers.

His trips in the pope mobile are also a sign of his interest in people. These rides are continually punctuated by baby-kissing interludes and tender moments with disabled children and adults. Clearly he values their presence in the Church. He even welcomed a seventeen-year-old boy with Down syndrome into the pope mobile, offering him a seat in the white papal chair.

Moments such as these reveal a man who is deeply committed to the diverse array of people under his care. They are not anonymous numbers or mere faces in a crowd but unique individuals, each called and gifted by God in a special way. As he said at the aforementioned press conference, "Everyone has to lead his own life, everyone has his own way of living and being."[120]

Francis was not giving his carte blanche blessing to those who would choose to live in a way contrary to God's law, but his words remind us that the members of Christ's body are not meant to be carbon copies of one another. For example, Pope Benedict was a world-class theologian and a skilled teacher who illuminated how faith and reason complement one another. He also vigorously addressed the abuse crisis and encouraged a return to reverence and beauty in the liturgy. Pope Francis brings a different set of gifts to the papacy, and his pontificate already exhibits a shift in emphasis. But this is as it should be. This is how the body of Christ thrives.

As Francis said in his address to the cardinals two days after his election:

> The Paraclete creates all the differences among the Churches, almost as if he were an Apostle of Babel. But on the other hand, it is he who creates unity from these differences, not in "equality" but in harmony. I remember the Father of the Church who described it thus: *Ipse harmonia est* [It is harmony itself]. The Paraclete, who gives different charisms to each of us, unites us in this community of the Church, that worships the Father, the Son, and Him, the Holy Spirit.[121]

But the Church is not just a community of individuals who have pooled their diverse talents for mutual benefit. It is a body with a head, from which it cannot be separated. It has a criterion for membership, a special mission, and a law to follow. The Holy Father has explained this in several of his general audiences.

Regarding the headship of Christ, he said:

> The image of the body helps us to understand this deep Church-Christ bond...this body has a head, Jesus, who guides, feeds and supports it...if the head is separated from the rest of the body, the whole person cannot survive. So it is in the Church, we must remain bound ever more deeply to Jesus...just as the body needs the lifeblood to keep it alive, so we must allow Jesus to work in us.[122]

The pope also sent out a tweet that summed this up: "One cannot separate Christ and the Church."[123]

As for membership in the body of Christ, Pope Francis has spoken about the importance of faith and baptism for the people of God: "It is through Baptism that we are introduced to this people, through faith in Christ, the gift of God which must be nurtured and tended to throughout our whole life."[124]

The mission of this people is, according to Pope Francis, "To bring to the world the hope and the salvation of God: to be a sign of the love of God who calls all to be friends of His; to be the yeast that ferments the dough, the salt that gives flavor and preserves from decay, the light that brightens."[125] The Holy Father clearly takes these words to heart every time he reaches out with a genuine spirit of goodwill to the multitudes who surround him. He is doing his part to be a sign of God's love.

This divine love is meant to guide the people of God. Francis reminds us that as members of the Church, we are called to follow "the law of love, love for God and love for our neighbor according to the new commandment that the Lord left us (see John 13:34)." Pope Francis insists that this love "is not sterile sentimentality or something vague." Rather, this love must be real and active, both recognizing God's primacy and also accepting other members of the body with a love that conquers "divisions, rivalry, misunderstandings, and selfishness."[126] This is the recipe for a healthy body. Indeed this unity is essential to the well-being of the body of Christ. Pope Francis has spoken passionately on this subject:

> Let us remember this well: being part of the Church means being united to Christ and receiving from Him the divine life that makes us live as Christians; it means remaining united to the Pope and the Bishops who are instruments of unity and communion, and also means overcoming personal interests and divisions, in order to understand each other better, to harmonize the variety and richness of each member; in a word, to love God and the people who are next to us more, in the family, in the parish, in the associations. In order to live a Body and its limbs must be united![127]

In the same general audience, the Holy Father addressed the unfortunate reality of factions within the Church. He does not condemn; rather he focuses on the solution. He exhorts us all to pray for the unity that comes from God:

> How much damage divisions among Christians, being partisan, narrow interests causes to the Church! Pray that the Lord gift us unity! Unity among ourselves! How will we ever have unity among Christians if we are not capable of

having it among us Catholics…. Seek unity, unity builds the Church and comes from Jesus Christ. He sends us the Holy Spirit to build unity!… Dear brothers and sisters, let us ask God to help us to be members of the Body of the Church always deeply united to Christ, help us not to hurt the Body of the Church with our conflicts, our divisions, selfishness: help us to be living members bound to each other by a single power, that of love, which the Holy Spirit pours into our hearts (cf. Rom 5:5).[128]

For Reflection: How Will I Respond?

Catechism of the Catholic Church 2030: "It is in the Church, in communion with all the baptized, that the Christian fulfills his vocation. From the Church he receives the Word of God containing the teachings of 'the law of Christ.' From the Church he receives the grace of the sacraments that sustains him on the 'way.' From the Church he learns the example of holiness and recognizes its model and source in the all-holy Virgin Mary; he discerns it in the authentic witness of those who live it; he discovers it in the spiritual tradition and long history of the saints who have gone before him and whom the liturgy celebrates in the rhythms of the sanctoral cycle."[129]

Consider: Of all the things the Church offers me, what do I find most valuable? What can I offer to the Church in return? How can the Church help me to deepen my knowledge of the law of Christ?

* * *

Pope Francis thinks of the Church as a mother, whose authority and guidance is always offered in a spirit of love. Without making a show of it, he has simply and sincerely adhered to her direction, identifying himself as "a son of the Church." Even when he has recognized places for growth in the Church, he has remained loyal nonetheless.

Consider: Do I appreciate the maternal authority of the Church? How loyal have I been to her? What could I do to help others understand the idea behind the title "Mother Church"?

* * *

St. Francis helped to reform the body of Christ, one member at a time. First by living the Gospel, and then by preaching it to others, he worked to keep the Bride of Christ healthy and beautiful. His individual efforts were usually on a small scale, but their long-term effects were enormous.

Consider: How often do I think about my role in and my influence on the entire body of Christ? Where can I grow in my Christian witness to others? How could I personally help to ensure the health of the Church?

CHAPTER FOUR
Peace

The Lord revealed to me this salutation, that we should say:
"The Lord give thee peace."[130]

—St. Francis

On the Cross Jesus knocked down the wall of enmity that
divides people and nations, and he brought reconciliation
and peace.[131]

—Pope Francis

St. Francis is famous for a prayer he didn't say. The popular
"Lord, make me a channel of your peace" made its first recorded
appearance in 1915, on the back of a holy card of St. Francis.[132]
Now the prayer has made its way onto the backs of some holy
cards of Pope Francis too. Regardless of who gets the credit, the
fact remains that both of these men have aspired to be channels
of peace.

A sincere Christian can hardly do otherwise. To follow Christ,
the Prince of Peace, is to receive the gift of peace in our hearts and
to embrace the call to peace with our neighbors. The latter flows
from the former. When we possess the peace of Christ, we too can
become channels, or instruments, of peace in the world. Indeed,
Jesus longed for us to live in true and lasting peace.

In the Gospels, we find two moments when Christ's desire for
peace is painted with intense emotional depth. The first is one
of the two occasions when we know for certain that Jesus wept.
Luke's Gospel describes Jesus's reaction as he looked at Jerusalem:

"And when he drew near and saw the city he wept over it, saying, 'Would that even today you knew the things that make for peace! But now they are hidden from your eyes'" (Luke 19:41–42). The lack of peace for the Jewish people was so tragic as to bring Christ to tears. Only the death of his friend Lazarus had a similar effect on Jesus's emotions (see John 11:35). For Christ, the lack of peace apparently resembles the sorrow of death.

The other moment when we catch a glimpse into Christ's heart-felt desire for peace among people is on the night of the Last Supper before his arrest. According to John's Gospel, after washing the disciples' feet, Jesus predicted the betrayal of Judas and the denial of Peter. Surprisingly, he followed these fateful announcements with consoling words. "Let not your hearts be troubled," he told the disciples, "believe in God; believe also in me" (John 14:1). Shortly thereafter he promised the gift of peace to his disciples, and again he urged them not to be disturbed: "Peace I leave with you; my peace I give to you; not as the world gives do I give to you. Let not your hearts be troubled, neither let them be afraid" (John 14:27).

Jesus concluded his farewell discourse by speaking specifically about peace amid trials: "I have said this to you, that in me you may have peace. In the world you have tribulation; but be of good cheer, I have overcome the world" (John 16:33).

On this sorrowful night, Jesus spoke not only about finding personal peace in him, even in the face of difficulty, but he also prayed for his disciples to be at peace with one another. Jesus "lifted up his eyes to heaven" and prayed to his Father on behalf of all his followers, present and future: "I do not pray for these only, but also for those who believe in me through their word, that they may all be one; even as you, Father, are in me, and I in you, that they also may be in us" (John 17:1, 20–21). These words stand as a sort of last will and testament that Christ made on the eve of his death, bequeathing divine peace and requesting unity among Christians.

After Christ's resurrection, in spite of his previous admonition not to be afraid, the disciples were hiding behind locked doors "for fear of the Jews." Jesus appeared to them and, as if recognizing their fear, greeted them by saying, "Peace be with you" (John 20:19). In his glorified state, of course, this was more than a friendly hello. This was a supernatural gift. Jesus said it again and then "breathed on them, and said to them, 'Receive the Holy Spirit'" (John 20:22).

This same Spirit is available to everyone through baptism, and with it comes, among other things, the gift of inner peace. St. Paul describes the fruits of the Holy Spirit in the book of Galatians: "But the fruit of the Spirit is love, joy, peace, patience, kindness, goodness, faithfulness, gentleness, self-control" (Galatians 5:22-23). Paul also writes that the Spirit of Christ brings "life and peace" (Romans 8:6) and that we should "let the peace of Christ rule in [our] hearts" (Colossians 3:15). He even describes the Good News of Jesus Christ as "the gospel of peace" (Ephesians 6:15).

This peace extends beyond ourselves. Thus the New Testament also emphasizes the importance of harmony among people. Jesus set the tone in his Sermon on the Mount. There, as part of the Beatitudes, Jesus declared, "Blessed are the peacemakers" (Matthew 5:9).

His sermon also teaches us to make a priority of being at peace with one another: "If you are offering your gift at the altar, and there remember that your brother has something against you, leave your gift there before the altar and go; first be reconciled to your brother, and then come and offer your gift" (Matthew 5:23). We lay the foundation for our very worship of God by approaching him in a state of peace.

St. Paul embraced and expounded upon the basic Gospel message. He urged the Church in Corinth, "Mend your ways, heed my appeal, agree with one another, live in peace, and the God of love and peace will be with you" (2 Corinthians 13:11). Elsewhere he emphasized that Christians should strive for peace even outside of their own communities. "If possible," he wrote, "so far as it depends upon you, live peaceably with all" (Romans 12:18).

As Christians we are called to believe that true peace is possible, through the power of Christ. Paul explains, "In Christ Jesus you who once were far off have been brought near in the blood of Christ. For he is our peace, who has made us both one, and has broken down the dividing wall of hostility" (Ephesians 2:13–14).

Indeed, Christ is our peace. The angels testified to this at the moment of his birth, with the celestial song we repeat to this day at Mass, "Glory to God in the highest, and peace to his people on earth!" (see Luke 2:14). Jesus "came and preached peace" (Ephesians 2:17) and gave us this peace through the gift of his Spirit. He forgave sinners, as he forgives us today, with the words "Go in peace" (Luke 7:50).

Our Francises both recognize the centrality of peace in the Christian faith. As we will see, they stand as witnesses to the power of Christ's peace in their hearts, and they have worked, each in his own way, to promote peace among people.

St. Francis and Peace in Our Hearts

Even in the face of poverty, humiliation, sickness, imprisonment, and rejection, St. Francis was ever at peace. He had left behind the comforts of the world, but in return he received the spiritual consolation of serving his divine master. This was enough for him. He had the inner peace that Christ alone can give. He spoke of how blessed we are to know Christ: "O how holy and how beloved, well pleasing and humble, peaceful and sweet and desirable above all to have such a brother who has laid down His life for His sheep, and who has prayed for us to the Father."[133]

Francis experienced peace in his heart because he was docile to Christ's Spirit. In his First Rule he expressed his belief that those who have the spirit of the Lord come to know "true peace of mind."[134] This kind of peace is not fleeting or superficial but persists through joys and sorrows, triumphs and trials. The most disturbing circumstances cannot ruffle this deep spiritual calm.

As a young man Francis became a prisoner of war during a battle between Assisi and the neighboring city of Perugia. During the course of nearly a year, while he waited for his father to ransom him, he experienced the beginning of his conversion to Christ. As he grew in love for the Lord, he received the gift of peace.

In the squalor of the jail cell, the other prisoners wallowed in sorrow and misery. But Francis was not downcast. He received divine consolation (some biographers suggest mystical visions) that convinced him that God had a beautiful plan for his life, in spite of its dismal appearance at that moment. As he told his fellow inmates when they questioned his happiness, "I will yet be venerated as a saint."[135]

Perhaps nowhere is this peace more evident than in the quiet way St. Francis handled the physical suffering of his final years. These included the wounds of the stigmata, which though bleeding and painful he kept carefully hidden. Not long after receiving these wounds of Christ, he began to lose his vision.

During this period of bodily weakness, in the year 1225, Francis retired to a hut at the monastery of San Damiano. There he composed his great hymn of praise to God, "The Canticle of the Sun." Not only is the composition a testament to Francis's personal peace, but it also speaks specifically about those who remain peaceful amid difficulty. To the original version of his magnificent poem, Francis later added this stanza:

> All praise be yours, my Lord through those who grant pardon
> for love of you; through those who endure sickness and trial.
> Happy those who endure in peace,
> By You, Most High, they will be crowned.[136]

Soon after writing the canticle, one of the brothers encouraged Francis to seek medical intervention for his eyes. Francis's encounter with the horrific medieval treatment for blindness reveals a remarkable degree of internal peace as well. The doctors resolved to cauterize his head. As the smoldering stakes were prepared, the patient was unruffled. With extraordinary peace and calm, Francis uttered these poetic words as the procedure began: "Brother Fire, God made you beautiful and strong and useful; I pray you be courteous with me."[137]

In his "Admonitions," Francis spoke about peace in the midst of pain with the authority of one who knows. He wrote: "'Blessed are the peacemakers; for they shall be called the children of God.' They are truly peacemakers who amidst all they suffer in this world maintain peace in soul and body for the love of our Lord Jesus Christ."[138] Francis understood that true peace was possible for those who love the Lord, regardless of what physical or spiritual trials may threaten that peace.

Pope Francis, during a visit to Assisi on October 4, 2013 (the feast of St. Francis), commented on the profound peace that his namesake possessed. "Many people when they think of St. Francis, think of peace," the Holy Father said. "Very few people, however, go deeper. What is the peace which Francis received, experienced and lived, and which he passes on to us? It is the peace of Christ, which is born of the greatest love of all, the love of the cross."[139]

St. Francis also understood that the inner peace of the individual was a necessary starting point for communal peace. If his preaching and that of the brothers were going to have any chance of success, they must start with their own internal peace and harmony. And so he told his little band of brothers, "As you preach peace by word, so you should also possess peace and superabundant peace in your hearts. Anger no one, nor vex any man: but by your meekness urge others to be peaceful, meek and merciful."[140]

Not only did Francis and the brothers preach and live peace, they also wished it to virtually everyone they met. Francis felt that the Lord had instructed him to use the same greeting of peace that was so popular among the early Christians. Indeed, the New Testament epistles are replete with greeting after greeting, wish after wish, for peace. And Francis saw to it that, for those who traveled the roads of thirteenth-century Italy, an encounter with one of the Friars Minor would mean hearing the words "May God give you peace."[141] He made this greeting obligatory among the brothers.

Those who had the good fortune to host one of these servants of Christ in their home would hear the words *"Peace to this house"* (see Luke 10:5),[142] because this too was required by Francis. And those who were so abundantly blessed as to hear a sermon preached by this man of peace would have heard him commence with the words "May the Lord give you His peace!"[143]

These persistent greetings were at times met with surprise, laughter, and even indignation. When one of the friars became somewhat intimidated by these unfavorable responses, he asked Francis if he could use some other greeting. "Heed them not," the saint replied, "for they know not what is of God. Be not ashamed of it, for the time will come when even the rich and princes of this world shall revere thee and thy brothers because of this greeting."[144]

Francis did what he could to be a witness to peace, to preach peace, and to wish peace on others. But more than all this, he also prayed for peace, trusting that Jesus would fulfill the promise he made to his disciples. Thus he blessed Brother Leo in the ancient words that many Christians still pray for one another today: "May the Lord bless thee and keep thee. May He shew His face to thee and have mercy on thee. May He turn His countenance to thee and give thee peace [see Numbers 6:24–26]."[145]

POPE FRANCIS AND PEACE IN OUR HEARTS

When our Holy Father Francis first appeared before the world on the balcony overlooking St. Peter's Square, most of us had never heard of him. Who was this man who stood before us, our new leader, so modest, so quiet, so unassuming? With no more movement than a slight, almost bashful wave of the hand, he silently looked out at the crowd.

The people, initially confused, gradually broke into wild cheering and shouts of "Viva il Papa!" Through it all Francis gazed quietly, appearing humble, meek, almost awkward. What was wrong? Shouldn't he be doing something? Didn't he know what to do? Couldn't he think of anything to say? Or was it possible this man was simply at peace?

Indeed, even on this momentous occasion, Pope Francis showed no need for the psychological support of ritual, convention, or spoken words. He appears to be a man who possesses true serenity, a man sustained by the peace of Christ.

Undoubtedly it would strike fear into the hearts of most of us to consider the immense task, the inimitable responsibility, of serving as supreme pontiff of the universal Church. The chamber in which a newly elected pope first dons his papal garb is called "the room of tears" for a reason. But from his first minutes, Pope Francis radiated a remarkable calm. He later said that, during lunch on March 13, 2013, before his election, he felt a wave of "deep and inexplicable inner peace and comfort" that remained with him. [146]

Within days of his election, he met with his longstanding acquaintance Cristina Fernandez de Kirchner, the president of Argentina. She reported that Pope Francis was "calm, confident and at peace, tranquil." [147] Perhaps this tranquility is a reflection of that peace of Christ that the Holy Father has called "the foundation and wellspring of apostolic courage and apostolic patience." [148] As then-Cardinal Bergoglio said in a retreat for bishops, this peace "enables us to choose a state of life and to do God's will."[149] In his case, doing God's will meant accepting his election as pope.

The fact that the task is daunting need not be cause for concern. As the cardinal said during the same retreat, "We are not talking about an easy peace, but rather a demanding one. Peace does not eliminate fragility or deficiencies.... It is not the peace the world gives but the peace of the Lord."[150]

Pope Francis insists that the peace of Christ is not about the absence of difficulties.

> We must not confuse true peace with the illusion of peace. This latter is the peace of ignorance, the peace of feigned innocence that dances around difficulties.... True peace grows out of the tension between two contrary elements: the acceptance of a present in which we recognize our weakness as sinners, and, at the same time, passing beyond the same present as if we were already freed from the burden of sin.[151]

We can have confidence in this peace from Christ because it is rooted in the victory that he already won for us through his cross and resurrection. "The greeting of the resurrected Christ, '*Peace be with you,*' is the watchword of definitive triumph. To participate in this peace, to receive it, means to participate already in the peace of the Resurrection," Pope Francis has said. [152] He also emphasizes that Christ desires to give us his peace. "The Lord consoles by making himself present in the midst of the community and showing his resurrected wounds, wounds flowing forth with peace, peace that conquers all fears."[153]

And so Jorge Bergoglio marches onward, like a valiant soldier following his orders from on high. "We step into combat with valor. We advance as 'victors,'" Bergoglio has said, because "we know that we can entrust all our worries to the Lord, since he always watches over us, even when the devil is prowling around us."[154]

For the Christian, this assurance of the Lord's protection and ultimate victory is the foundation on which peace is built in the heart. "The locus of this peace is the heart," the Holy Father has told us. "It is here that the presence of Jesus gives us assurance."[155]

In order to welcome Jesus's presence within us, we need to be sure we are prepared to receive him. During a Lenten homily, Cardinal Bergoglio encouraged the faithful, "Return to God: let yourself be reconciled with God. Do not harden your heart; listen to the voice of the Lord. Make a place in your hearts by means of prayer, penance, and almsgiving so that our Lord will come to you."[156]

When we ready ourselves for the Lord's presence, we will surely find it. Francis assures us, "Whoever is disposed to receive the Lord with all his heart will be able to know and follow the Lord. On the other hand, hearts that are inattentive, distracted, and superficial, focused on anything but the essential, kill the desire for God and his mystery."[157]

And what is essential? As always, Pope Francis brings us back to Christ. In his message for the Year of Faith, he explained how we let go of fear by welcoming Jesus:

> One passes through the door of faith, one crosses that threshold, when the Word of God is announced and the heart allows itself to be shaped by that transformative grace—a grace which has a concrete name: and that name is Jesus.... Jesus is the door, and he knocks on our door so that we might allow him to cross the threshold of our lives. "Be

not afraid...open wide the doors for Christ!" Blessed John Paul II told us at the beginning of his papacy. We must open the doors of our hearts.[158]

When Jesus reigns in our hearts, we can experience the gift of peace he won for us.

> Our God is the God of peace. He desired to give us this peace, by pacifying us in his Son.... The advent of this peace was made known to all on Christmas Eve, and the echo of this announcement resounds all the way to Palm Sunday. We have been asked to seek it, and to direct our feet "*into the way of peace*," for all of us have been called to live in peace. May this peace guard our hearts and minds and inspire us to seek peace with all men and women.[159]

ST. FRANCIS AND PEACE WITH OUR NEIGHBOR

Not only a man of peace, St. Francis was a maker of peace among men. He required peace among the brothers, taking his lead from the teachings of Jesus. Using the Gospels as his basis, Francis instructed the friars thus:

> There must be no quarrelling among themselves or with others, and they should be content to answer everyone humbly, saying, *We are unprofitable servants* (Luke 17:10). They must not give way to anger because the Gospel says: *Everyone who is angry with his brother shall be liable to judgment; and whoever says to his brother "Raca," shall be liable to the Sanhedrin; and whoever says, "Thou fool!" shall be liable to the fire of Gehenna* (Matthew 5:22).[160]

But his contributions to harmony between people went beyond the members of his order. The stories of towns and villages benefitting from the peacemaking skills of Francis and his friars are plentiful.

For example, Assisi was in bitter turmoil in the year 1210, as the *majores* and the *minores* battled over the question of expanded rights for the *minores*. When Francis returned from Rome, he and his band settled nearby and became aware of the squabbling. So each Saturday night, Francis would walk into Assisi, spend the night in a hut in the canon's garden, and on Sunday morning preach on peace, forgiveness, and reconciliation at the Cathedral of San Rufino. The topic was judiciously chosen to address the civic unrest.

His efforts met with success. On November 9, 1210, the nobles and the citizens of Assisi signed a peace pact. The feudal lords granted full equal rights to their subjects.

Again, in Bologna there was a longstanding feud between the nobles. Francis arrived there on the Feast of the Assumption in 1222. Before nearly all the townspeople on the public square, he spoke of laying down arms and making covenants of peace. Even the most determined enemies could not remain locked in combat when confronted by the holiness of a man like Francis. The warring families abruptly laid aside their differences.

On another occasion Francis used an innovative method to procure peace. Arriving at the city of Arezzo, he found the rich and the poor at each other's throats. Complete destruction of the city seemed inevitable. So great was the chaos that Francis decided to lodge outside the city.

There Francis saw a vision of devils rejoicing over the hostility and raising up the citizens against one another. So Francis summoned Brother Sylvester and instructed, "Go before the gate of the city, and on the part of the Almighty God command the devils to leave the city as quickly as they can."[161]

Sylvester courageously followed the instruction. Shortly thereafter the city returned to a state of peace and tranquility, with the poor preserving their civic rights.

Back in his hometown of Assisi, Francis was a force for peace on yet another occasion. On his return from a journey, Francis learned that the city magistrate—the *podesta*—and the bishop were in conflict. The bishop excommunicated the *podesta*, who in turn made it illegal for anyone to interact with the bishop. Saddened by news of the standoff, Francis told his brothers, "It is a great shame for us, God's servants, that no one makes peace here."[162]

Francis took matters into his own hands. He managed to arrange a meeting between the adversaries, and in the meantime, he composed the extra stanza about peace for his "Canticle of the Sun." When the bishop and *podesta* arrived, two friars stepped up to sing the canticle, complete with the new addition about giving pardon for the love of God and enduring in peace.

The strategy worked. The magistrate forgave the bishop, as he said, "out of love to our Lord Jesus Christ and to his servant Francis,"[163] and the bishop begged forgiveness for being inclined to anger.

Another bold attempt at peace deserves mention, though it did not meet with the success to which Francis was accustomed. In the year 1219, during the Fifth Crusade, Francis traveled to Egypt and crossed enemy lines to meet with Malik al-Kamil, the Muslim sultan of Egypt. Francis wanted to tell the sultan about

Jesus and convert him to Christianity by means of evangelization instead of the sword. The sultan, unlike some in his camp who had insulted and beaten Francis earlier, welcomed the Christian saint and listened to him respectfully. The sultan didn't convert and the crusade didn't end, but Francis gave a powerful witness to the virtually unheard-of practice of interreligious dialogue. On his return home he expressed his desire that the friars live in peace with Muslims.

Perhaps Francis's most notable achievement in the practice of making peace was a simple but inspired act that may well rank among the most astute and significant peacemaking efforts in history. It was an act that brought about widespread social reform. In essence, Francis trumped the feudal system, with its practices of vassalage and local warfare, by establishing this rule for lay members of the Third Order:

> The brothers may not receive arms to be wielded against any person, nor bear them on their person. Let all refrain from taking solemn oaths, except in those instances decreed by the Pope; namely where peace, the Faith, or a juridical oath is at stake.... If the Brothers and Sisters are troubled contrary to their right and privilege, or by the rulers of the places where they abide, let their own prefects together with the Lord Bishop resort to measures which may appear to them proper.[164]

Because members of the Third Order were technically religious and not laymen, this provision did not put them at odds with the law. They were subject only to Church authority.

Of course, the nobles opposed this, demanding adherence to the traditional oath of fealty that required subjects to take up arms at their lord's command. But on December 16, 1221, Pope Honorius III officially gave tertiaries exemption from the oath. Thus the floodgates were opened. Seeking to free themselves from military obligations in this roundabout way, the faithful flocked to Francis in large numbers. Within thirty years, half of Italy marched peacefully under the Franciscan banner.

Pope Francis and Peace with Our Neighbor

Between 1976 and 1983, Argentina was ruled by a military dictatorship that was ruthless in stamping out opposition. Thousands upon thousands of politicians, teachers, students, writers, trade unionists, and pregnant women (whose babies were stolen and given to military families without children) were imprisoned, were killed, were tortured, or just disappeared. These were the horrible conditions under which Jorge Bergoglio worked to foster peace.

During much of this period, Fr. Jorge served as provincial of the Society of Jesus in Argentina. His was the task of maintaining a delicate balance between keeping his priests safe and responding to the needs of the laypeople oppressed by the government. Some of his priests wanted to fight. Fr. Jorge, while acknowledging their feelings, was clear in teaching that priests must not succumb to such temptations.

> [Christ] unequivocally rejects recourse to violence. The perspective of His mission is much deeper. It consists in complete salvation through transforming, peacemaking, pardoning, reconciling love. There is no doubt that all this is very demanding for the attitude of the Christian who wishes

to truly serve his least brethren, the poor, the needy, the emarginated; in a word, all those who in their lives reflect the sorrowing face of the Lord.[165]

As Vatican spokesman, Fr. Federico Lombardi said of the Holy Father, "He has always rejected violence, saying that its price is always paid by the weakest."[166]

Bergoglio has constantly been unabashed in his public calls for peace. At a *Te Deum* Mass in Argentina, he boldly confronted the tendency to be "quick to intolerance" warning that "copying the hate and violence of the tyrant and the murderer is the best way to inherit it."[167]

Now his voice for peace echoes far beyond the borders of Argentina. And unfortunately, within the first half of his first year as pope, the Holy Father had ample opportunity to make himself heard on the subject. With the outbreak of civil war in Syria and the use of chemical weapons that followed, Pope Francis found himself confronted yet again with a tragically violent situation. At his Angelus address on September 1, 2013, the pope made a passionate and eloquent plea for peace, particularly with regard to the conflict in Syria:

> Today, dear brothers and sisters, I wish to add my voice to the cry which rises up with increasing anguish from every part of the world, from every people, from the heart of each person, from the one great family which is humanity: it is the cry for peace! It is a cry which declares with force: we want a peaceful world, we want to be men and women of peace, and we want in our society, torn apart by divisions and conflict, that peace break out! War never again! Never

again war!... With all my strength, I ask each party in this conflict to listen to the voice of their own conscience, not to close themselves in solely on their own interests, but rather to look at each other as brothers and decisively and courageously to follow the path of encounter and negotiation, and so overcome blind conflict. With similar vigor I exhort the international community to make every effort to promote clear proposals for peace in that country without further delay, a peace based on dialogue and negotiation, for the good of the entire Syrian people.[168]

And then he proposed something that had never been done before:

To this end, brothers and sisters, I have decided to proclaim for the whole Church on 7 September next, the vigil of the birth of Mary, Queen of Peace, a day of fasting and prayer for peace in Syria, the Middle East, and throughout the world, and I also invite each person, including our fellow Christians, followers of other religions and all men of good will, to participate, in whatever way they can, in this initiative. On 7 September, in St. Peter's Square, here, from 7 p.m. until 12 a.m., we will gather in prayer and in a spirit of penance, invoking God's great gift of peace upon the beloved nation of Syria and upon each situation of conflict and violence around the world. Humanity needs to see these gestures of peace and to hear words of hope and peace! I ask all the local churches, in addition to fasting, that they gather to pray for this intention.[169]

Making St. Peter's Square the site for a peace vigil was unprecedented for the Vatican. And it was a marked success. One hundred thousand people responded to the pope's invitation and gathered for prayer. They also heard the Holy Father's passionate exhortations for peace.

> This evening I ask the Lord that we Christians, and our brothers and sisters of other religions and every man and woman of good will, cry out forcefully: Violence and war are never the way to peace! May the noise of weapons cease! War always marks the failure of peace, it is always a defeat for humanity.[170]

In solidarity with those gathered in Rome, bishops around the world declared fasts and vigils. In Argentina, people gathered in Buenos Aires's *Plaza de Mayo* and in other cities as well. Different areas of Italy and Cuba were also reported to have joined in the effort.

And the ripples extended beyond Christian circles. Even the Grand Mufti of Syria—the spiritual leader of Sunni Islam—thanked Pope Francis and encouraged Muslims to participate in the fast. "This is already a success," said a Hindu named Anata who attended the St. Peter's event, "the fact that all of us are here, Hindus, Christians, Buddhists, atheists."[171] It was also apparently a success because, within three days of the vigil, Syria astounded the world by agreeing to place its chemical weapons under international control.

Fostering such unity among people of diverse religious backgrounds is another element of Pope Francis's peacemaking efforts. He has reached out to Jews and Muslims in particular in several ways. He collaborated with the World Jewish Congress, for example, to establish Tzedakah, a Catholic-Jewish organization, whose goal is to support the poor. He and his friend

Rabbi Abraham Skorka jointly published a book recounting their conversations on God, religion, politics, the Holocaust, abortion, poverty, money, science, same-sex marriage, interreligious dialogue, and other topics. In that book the Holy Father emphasized the importance of dialogue and the interior landscape that gives birth to it:

> Dialogue is born from a respectful attitude toward the other person, from a conviction that the other person has something good to say. It supposes that we can make room in our heart for their point of view, their opinion and their proposals. Dialogue entails a warm reception and not a preemptive condemnation. To dialogue, one must know how to lower the defenses, to open the doors of one's home and to offer warmth.[172]

He also spoke of the interior attitudes and flaws that impede dialogue, such as "domination, not knowing how to listen, annoyance in our speech, preconceived judgments."

> There are very many barriers in everyday life that impede dialogue: misinformation, gossip, prejudices, defamation, and slander. All of these realities make up a certain cultural sensationalism that drowns out any possibility of openness to others. Thus, dialogue and encounter falter.[173]

Pope Francis has practiced what he preaches. In Argentina, he undertook a decade-long effort to encourage positive dialogue between Muslims and Christians. His work was described as "significant in the history of monotheistic relations in Argentina" by the Secretary General of the Islamic Center of the Argentine

Republic, Dr. Sumer Noufouri.[174] But more than just talking about interfaith cooperation, then-Archbishop Bergoglio opened the metropolitan cathedral in Buenos Aires several times for inter-religious prayer services. In November 2012 he invited leaders of different faith traditions to the cathedral to pray for peace in the Middle East.

Pope Francis continues to offer prayers for the Middle East and for the entire world. In fact, he made a point of entrusting all nations to the care of Mary, whom he has invoked as the Queen of Peace. Thus, following in the footsteps of Pope John Paul II, the Holy Father consecrated the whole world to the Immaculate Heart of Mary on October 13, 2013. Clearly, Francis believes that Mary desires to intercede for all people to promote the cause for peace.

FOR REFLECTION: HOW WILL I RESPOND?

Catechism of the Catholic Church 2305: "Earthly peace is the image and fruit of the peace of Christ, the messianic 'Prince of Peace.' By the blood of his Cross, 'in his own person he killed the hostility,' he reconciled men with God and made his Church the sacrament of the unity of the human race and of its union with God. 'He is our peace.' He has declared: 'Blessed are the peacemakers.'"

Consider: When, if ever, have I experienced "the peace of Christ" in my life? Where do I stand in regard to being reconciled with God? With others? With myself? Am I a peacemaker?

* * *

St. Francis was not troubled by his troubles. His breach with his father, his imprisonment, and his poor health did not defeat him.

Why? Because he was open to the spirit of the Lord that brings what he called "true peace of mind."

Consider: How do I respond to trials and challenges? How often do I fret or become anxious about these situations? How could I open myself to the Holy Spirit in these moments? What spiritual resolution could I make to nurture peace of mind?

* * *

Pope Francis, while never wavering in his own Catholic identity, nonetheless appreciates encountering people of other faiths. Instead of approaching such situations with a defensive attitude, the Holy Father begins with the assumption that "the other person has something good to say." This wards off conflict, and paves the way for peaceful, fruitful dialogue.

Consider: What are my thoughts about people of different faiths than my own? Do I open myself to their point of view, their perspective, and their proposals? How could I establish peace in my interactions with those whose opinion I do not share?

CHAPTER FIVE

Joy

In my presence and in the presence of others, try to be always joyful, for it is not fitting that a servant of God appear before the brothers or other men with a sad and glum face.[175]

—St. Francis

The encounter with the living Jesus…fills the heart with joy, because it fills it with true life, a profound goodness that does not pass away or decay.[176]

—Pope Francis

St. Francis called himself God's court jester—the *Jongleur de Dieu*—as he went about singing the praise of God. Pope Francis brought the house down the night of his election, telling his brother cardinals, "May God forgive you!"[177]

One can't help but notice a kind of effervescent joy that spreads happiness to others. These men have shattered the stereotype of rigid, grim, calcified piety. They radiate something entirely different: the joy of Christ.

Jesus was attractive, in the literal sense of the word. People wanted to meet him and hear him and follow him. St. Francis had a similar effect, and if the three million people who showed up at World Youth Day in Rio de Janeiro are any indication, Pope Francis does too. The wisdom and faith of these men make them intriguing, to be sure, but their spirit of joy goes a long way in drawing these crowds.

Christians, of course, are supposed to be joyful (and attractive, for that matter). As mentioned in the last chapter, one of the fruits of the Holy Spirit is joy. St. Paul prayed for believers, "May the God of hope fill you with all joy and peace in believing" (Romans 15:13).

Joy and peace appear to be at their best when they come in tandem. If peace is an absence of turmoil, strife, and discontent, joy is the presence of delight, fulfillment, and happiness. Though peace is no guarantee of joy, joy cannot subsist without peace.

But Christians have access to both. At the very "birth" of the faith, on the night of the Lord's Nativity, the angel announced not only peace to men on earth but joy as well: "I bring you good news of a great joy which will come to all the people" (Luke 2:10). Indeed, "The kingdom of God...[means] peace and joy in the Holy Spirit" (Romans 14:17).

The good news of the Gospel, the cause of Christian joy, is that this kingdom of God "is at hand" (Mark 1:15). Jesus declared that he "was sent for this purpose," to "preach the good news of the kingdom of God" (Luke 4:3). He told us, "The kingdom of God is in your midst" (Luke 17:21). Through our baptism, we are members of royalty, and that is cause for rejoicing!

But Jesus's kingdom doesn't operate like an earthly one; his kingdom "is not of this world" (John 18:36). Thus, as opposed to the usual riches and power promised kings and queens, Jesus speaks about poverty and persecution: "Blessed are you poor, for yours is the kingdom of God" (Luke 6:20), and "Blessed are those who are persecuted for righteousness' sake, for theirs is the kingdom of heaven" (Matthew 5:10). How strange that there should be a blessing in all of this! Yet this joy in the midst of suffering is part of what Christ won for us on the cross. As it says in the book of Hebrews, Jesus "for the joy that was set before him endured the cross, despising its shame, and is seated at the right hand of the throne of God" (Hebrews 12:2).

One of the greatest gifts of the Christian faith is the ability to unite our (inevitable) sufferings to those of Christ and thus share in his glory. He told his followers, "Truly, truly, I say to you, you will weep and lament, but the world will rejoice; you will be sorrowful, but your sorrow will turn into joy…. So you have sorrow now; but I will see you again and your hearts will rejoice, and no one will take your joy from you" (John 16:20, 22).

Christians believe that through Christ we can find joy in the crosses we must carry in our lives. Not only are we able to bear them, but we can actually rejoice in them! Jesus told us as much when he said, "Blessed are you when men hate you, and when they exclude you and revile you, and cast out your name as evil, on account of the Son of Man. Rejoice in that day, and leap for joy, for behold, your reward is great in heaven; for so their fathers did to the prophets" (Luke 6:22–23).

St. Francis had a habit of leaping for joy at the most unexpected moments, and Pope Francis speaks clearly of the reality of joy even in the cross. In this, they resemble the early Christians. The New Testament epistles refer time and again to being joyful during persecution:

> Rejoice in the Lord always; again I will say, Rejoice. Let all men know your forbearance. The Lord is at hand. Have no anxiety about anything, but in everything by prayer and supplication with thanksgiving let your requests be made known to God. And the peace of God, which passes

all understanding, will keep your hearts and your minds in Christ Jesus. (Philippians 4:4–7)

Rejoice always, pray constantly, give thanks in all circumstances; for this is the will of God in Christ Jesus for you. (1 Thessalonians 5:16–18)

Count it all joy, my brethren, when you meet various trials. (James 1:2)

Beloved, do not be surprised at the fiery ordeal which comes upon you to prove you, as though something strange were happening to you. But rejoice in so far as you share Christ's sufferings, that you may also rejoice and be glad when his glory is revealed. (1 Peter 4:12)

The early Church didn't just talk about joy in trial; she experienced it. After some important and influential Jews threw Paul and Barnabas out, "the disciples were filled with joy and with the Holy Spirit" (Acts 13:52). When the Christians in Macedonia faced affliction, "their abundance of joy…overflowed" (2 Corinthians 8:2). The Thessalonians "received the word in much affliction, with joy inspired by the Holy Spirit" (1 Thessalonians 1:6).

Jesus, too, "rejoiced in the Holy Spirit" (Luke 10:21). And he wanted us to share in his joy. "These things I have spoken to you," Jesus told his disciples, "that my joy may be in you, and that your joy may be full" (John 15:11). Twice again Jesus speaks in these terms: "Ask, and you will receive, that your joy may be full" (John 16:24), and, "These things I speak in the world, that they may have my joy fulfilled in themselves" (John 17:13).

This fullness of joy is our inheritance as Christians. And it doesn't always have to come with suffering! The gift of knowing Christ, being subjects of the King of Kings, is a great joy in and of itself. This is what Jesus taught: "The kingdom of heaven is like treasure hidden in a field, which a man found and covered up; then in his joy he goes and sells all that he has and buys that field" (Matthew 13:44).

St. Francis and Pope Francis have given everything, dedicating their entire lives for the sake of the kingdom of heaven. And in this they have found great joy.

St. Francis and Joy in the Cross

"I announce to you a great joy and an unprecedented miracle,"[178] wrote Brother Elias several days after the death of Francis. "Shortly before his death our father and brother appeared to us crucified: his body displayed the five wounds which are truly the stigmata of Christ."[179]

How remarkable that something so physically painful as the stigmata should be proclaimed with "great joy." But in the spirit of their founder, the Franciscans did in fact rejoice in the news. The marks of the Lord's passion imprinted on Francis's hands and side confirmed for his followers that he was intimately conformed to Christ. And for Francis, the suffering these wounds entailed, along with the manifold other physical ailments he endured in the last years of his life, were cause for joy.

In a humble hermitage on Mount La Verna, the holy saint received this final seal of his imitation of Christ. Brother Leo, who was there with Francis, gives us his testimony of the event:

Two years before his death, blessed Francis was fasting in the place called La Verna.... And the hand of the Lord was upon him. After the vision and words of the seraph and the impression of the stigmata of Christ in his body, he composed the praises written on the other side of this small piece of parchment. He wrote them in his own hand giving thanks to God for the benefit which had been granted him.[180]

The stigmata a benefit? To bleed continually from five places for two years, a cause for praising and thanking God? What explains the ability to find joy while suffering under the weight of the cross?

For Francis the joy was in suffering for the sake of heaven. He found comfort in a revelation that occurred when he was near death and confined to total darkness because of the pain light caused to his eyes. "Rejoice," came the voice, "Rejoice as if you already shared my kingdom."[181]

This divine word confirmed what Francis had written years earlier: "We should be glad when we *fall into various trials* (James 1:2), and when we suffer anguish of soul or body, or affliction of any kind in this world, for the sake of life eternal."[182]

"Rejoice and be glad," Francis seems to tell us. Our earthly sufferings, which soon pass, make reparation for sin and pave the way for a heaven of unspeakable joy that never ends!

Not only can suffering yield such marvelous fruit, but for Francis there was another reason to rejoice in trials. He believed that affliction was actually a sign of God's love. He instructed the brothers to give thanks in the midst of trial.

I beg the friar who is sick to thank God for everything; he should be content to be as God wishes him to be, in sickness or in health, because it is those *"who were destined for eternal life"* (Acts 13:48) that God instructs by sickness and affliction and the spirit of compunction. He tells us Himself, *"those whom I love I rebuke and chastise"* (Revelation 3:19).[183]

The brothers took up these lessons and made them central to their ministry. In *The Legend of the Three Companions*, we read of some shabby treatment the brothers endured in the city of Florence:

> The brothers suffered all this, hunger, thirst, cold, naked-ness, and many immense tribulations, firmly and patiently, as St. Francis had bidden them. They were not dejected, they never cursed their tormentors; but like men whose faces are set to a great reward they exulted in tribulations and joyfully prayed to God for their persecutors.[184]

Indeed, for Francis, taking up the cross was a continual *source* of joy! His life, which was at the same time a life of joyous celebration and a life of self-imposed poverty and penance, proves this.

Consider the first time he begged for food. His efforts yielded a bowl containing such an unappetizing assortment of scraps that his stomach turned at the thought of eating them. But when for love of God he forced himself to eat, the scraps seemed to him the most delicious food in the world. In fact, "His heart leaped with joy and he thanked God, for he realized that, though weak and afflicted in body, he was able to endure anything, however hard, for love of the Lord. He praised and thanked God who had changed what was bitter into sweetness."[185]

St. Francis was a tangible manifestation of the paradox of the cross. Suffering brings salvation. Death ends in life. Sorrow leads to joy. His life revealed the truth of the counterintuitive promises Christ made in the Beatitudes. As St. Paul wrote, "Has not God made foolish the wisdom of the world?" (1 Corinthians 1:20). This is precisely what Francis did too by casting off the ways of the world with such supernatural glee.

G.K. Chesterton believed that Francis outwitted the world:

> You could not threaten to starve a man who was ever striving to fast. You could not ruin him and reduce him to beggary, for he was already a beggar. There was a very lukewarm satisfaction even in beating him with a stick, when he only indulged in little leaps and cries of joy because indignity was his only dignity.[186]

This last image calls to mind Francis's famous teaching to Brother Leo on perfect joy.

> As the two were walking along the road near the Portiuncula Francis said, "Brother Leo, write down what is perfect joy. If a messenger should arrive from Paris to announce that all of the teachers at the great university had joined the Order, write down this would not be perfect joy. If all the prelates and the bishops and the kings of France and England should join the Order, write down this would not be perfect joy. If all the friars should go among the infidels and convert them to the true faith or if I should cure all the sick and work many miracles, write down this would not be perfect joy."
>
> "Pray tell, Father Francis," Leo inquired, "what then is perfect joy?"

"If we return from Perugia in the black of night," the saint continued, "and it is winter and cold and there is mud and ice cycles are hanging from the hems of our tunics and they strike our legs which are bloody and sore and we arrive at the door of the Portiuncula frozen and weary; if we knock at the door desperate and starving and we are told, 'Begone you worthless scoundrels, this is no hour to be wandering about!'; if we knock again saying, 'It is I Brother Francis and Leo,' and we are told, 'Don't come here, we do not want you!' and we insist saying, 'For the love of God give us shelter for we are frozen and hungry,' and again we are told to go away; if we persist and knock again pleading for mercy and the porter comes out and drags us through the ice and snow beyond reach of the door and says, 'Go away you miserable wretches and do not come back for you are vile and we do not want you here!'; if we endure all this with patience and cheerfulness, in that, I say to you, Brother Leo, lies perfect joy."[187]

Francis understood that where there is perfect joy, at least on this earth, there also is the cross.

POPE FRANCIS AND JOY IN THE CROSS

Jorge Bergoglio is no stranger to suffering. At the age of twenty-one, his life hung in the balance because of a severe lung infection. As he lay delirious with fever, he pleaded desperately with his mother, "Tell me, what's happening to me?"[188] But she had no answer.

Eventually pneumonia and three cysts were discovered, and a portion of his lung had to be removed. He endured excruciating pain for several days, as saline was pumped through his system and a drainage tube was connected to his chest. In the midst of all this, friends and family members attempted to assure him that it would all pass and encouraged him to think about returning home. But none of these expressions of sympathy consoled him.

It was not until the nun who had prepared him for his First Communion, Sr. Dolores, came to visit him that he felt relief. "You are imitating Christ," she said.[189]

This thought brought the young Jorge comfort in the midst of his suffering. That experience of being like Christ, even in his suffering, has helped shape the Holy Father's teachings on the cross.

"The key," Pope Francis has said, "is to understand the cross as the seed of resurrection. Any attempt to cope with pain will bring partial results, if it is not based in transcendence. It is a gift to understand and fully live through pain."[190] He has also explained:

> The cross is only meaningful for those of us who believe in eternal life. For the one who does not believe in eternal life but instead believes that all that exists is created here and ends here, and lives as though this were true, for him the cross bears no meaning...nor does he understand it as the triumph of God's salvation of us all.[191]

On September 14, the Feast of the Triumph of the Cross, we celebrate the fact that suffering has been redeemed by Christ. For the Christian, trial and tribulation end in triumph. This realization gives us reason to be joyful in our suffering. "Christian life is bearing witness with cheerfulness, as Jesus did," the pope has said.[192]

A report on one of the pope's homilies elaborates:

> Pope Francis said even in troubling times, Christians are full
> of joy and never sad, like Paul and Silas who were perse-
> cuted and imprisoned for witnessing to the Gospel. They
> were joyful, he said, because they followed Jesus on the path
> of his passion....
>
> The Pope recalled that so many martyrs were joyful, such
> as the martyrs of Nagasaki who helped each other, as they
> "waited for the moment of death." Pope Francis recalled of
> some martyrs that "they went to martyrdom" as if they were
> going to a "wedding party." This attitude of endurance,
> he added, is a Christian's normal attitude, but it is not a
> masochistic attitude. It is an attitude that leads them "along
> the path of Jesus."[193]

As Christians, we challenge the wisdom of the world by finding
joy in suffering. But even more than that, we totally defy worldly
logic by voluntarily taking on suffering through fasting and
penance. "You can fast and put yourself through other forms of
deprivation and continue your spiritual progress, without sacri-
ficing peace and cheerfulness," Pope Francis tells us. [194]

Although we seek to be joyful in the midst of suffering, the pope
rightly reminds us that we are not masochists. We do not regard
suffering as an innate good. "Pain is not a virtue in itself," the
pope says. [195] There are times when we should avoid suffering: We
seek medical assistance, and St. Francis sought to ease the pain of
the brother "dying of hunger." There are also times when we are
called to persevere in suffering. And when we freely elect to take
on suffering, it is for a purpose, such as developing self-discipline
or making reparation for sin.

When Jesus made it clear to his disciples that he would have to go to Jerusalem and suffer greatly, Peter tried to rebuke him, saying, "God forbid, Lord! This shall never happen to you" (Matthew 16:22). Jesus then rebuked Peter: "Get behind me, Satan! You are a hindrance to me; for you are not on the side of God, but of men" (Matthew 16:23). The pope reflected on this in a homily he gave to the cardinals:

> The same Peter who professed Jesus Christ now says to him:… I will follow you, but let us not speak of the Cross. That has nothing to do with it. I will follow you on other terms, but without the Cross. When we journey without the Cross, when we build without the Cross, when we profess Christ without the Cross, we are not disciples of the Lord, we are worldly: we may be bishops, priests, cardinals, popes, but not disciples of the Lord.[196]

Pope Francis understands that Christians have a fundamental responsibility to accept, even embrace, the cross. But too often we recoil from this obligation. Thus he has rightly rebuked us, indeed rebuked the entire Church:

> The temptation for the Church has been and will always be the same: to avoid the cross (see Matthew 16:22), compromise the truth, diminish the redemptive power of Christ's Cross to escape persecution. Oh wretched, lukewarm church that shuns and avoids the cross![197]

The cross cannot be shunned if we are to follow Christ. However, this does not mean that we are destined to become miserable or hopeless. The question is really how we will respond to the inevitable crosses in our lives. Harboring bitterness only makes matters worse:

> Resentment is bitterness.... Resentment is like a house where squatters live piled one atop another with no view of the sky. While pain is also like a house where there are a lot of people living on top of one another, but you can still see the sky. In other words, pain is open to prayer, to affection, to the company of a friend, to a thousand things that give an individual dignity. Pain is a healthier condition.[198]

Yet the pain is not the end of the story for those who are open to God's presence within their suffering. As Pope Francis assures us, "If we wish to follow Christ closely, we cannot choose an easy, quiet life. It will be a demanding life, but full of joy."[199]

St. Francis and Joy in the Kingdom of God

St. Francis didn't need the cross to find joy. After his love for poverty, St. Francis's joyful nature was perhaps his most evident characteristic. He was a cheerful, friendly, and spontaneous man.

As a youth, he immersed himself in the pleasure-loving life of the village. Feasts, banquets, jousts, and ceremonial processions were the order of the day, and Francis, who was always chosen to enjoy the honor of serving as "king of the feasts," was what we would call today the life of the party. But at times a sense of emptiness came upon him after the festivities. King though he may have been, in this social kingdom, he did not find the fullness of joy.

Francis sought to give purpose to his existence by arming himself as a knight. He decided to pursue adventure and fame battling for the papal forces in Apulia. In a dream on the night before his departure, he saw his father's house filled with saddles, armor, and other knightly trappings. In one room of the house a beautiful bride was awaiting her bridegroom. Francis awoke filled with joy, thinking that this foreshadowed the worldly success he was destined to achieve.

But his adventure ended prematurely. After setting out for battle, he received another vision in which God told him, "Return to your own country. There it shall be revealed to you what you are to do, and you will come to understand the meaning of this vision."[200] The process of finding his true vocation had begun.

The townsfolk were amazed to find that Francis did not seem humiliated by this apparent failure upon his return. Instead he seemed more joyful than ever. True joy—joy strong in the face of adversity, joy based upon service to the King of kings—was beginning to take root.

A significant turning point came in 1206, when Francis redirected his noble aspirations by declaring himself in the service of the Lord, espoused to his Lady Poverty. On being accosted by robbers and asked who he was, he joyously replied, "I am the herald of the great King. What is that to you?"[201]

Not impressed by his answer, the villains beat him and cast him into a snow-filled ditch. After they left, Francis rose out of the ditch, shook off the snow, and joyfully began to praise God out loud.

Indeed, joy was at the heart of Francis's life and ministry. He expected it of the brothers as well. "They should let it be seen that they are happy in God, cheerful and courteous, as is expected of them, and be careful not to appear gloomy or depressed like hypocrites."[202]

When a companion displayed a downcast face, Francis admonished him, "Why do you display the sadness and sorrow that you feel for your sins that way? It is a matter between you and God. Pray to him that in his goodness he give you the joy of salvation."[203]

Francis took his own advice. When he was tempted toward despair or dejection, he would pray at once. "If the servant of God, as may happen, is disturbed in any way," Francis said, "he should rise immediately to pray and he should remain in the presence of the heavenly Father until he *restores unto him the joy of salvation.*"[204]

Along with prayer, Francis had recourse to music and song to bring cheer to body and soul. In fact, music played no small role in the life of the order. Many talented troubadours joined and lent their talents to joyfully singing the praises of God. This helps explain the popularity of the brethren at a time when music and poetry were such an integral part of the culture. Toward the end of his life, Francis said of the Friars Minor, "For what are God's servants but his minstrels...who must inspire the hearts of men and stir them to spiritual joy."[205]

A perfect example of the joy that comes of praising God is St. Francis's literary masterpiece, "The Canticle of the Sun." These joyous words, for which he also composed a melody, have been called "the most ancient and precious jewel of Italian poetry."[206] Francis sang:

> Most high, all-powerful, all good, Lord!
>> All praise is yours, all glory, all honour
>> And all blessing.
> To you alone, Most High, do they belong.
>> No mortal lips are worthy

To pronounce your name.

All praise be yours, my Lord, through all that you have made,

    And first my lord Brother Sun,

    Who brings the day; and light you give to us through him.

How beautiful is he, how radiant in all his splendor!

    Of you, Most High, he bears the likeness.

All praise be yours, my Lord, through Sister Moon and Stars;

    In the heavens you have made them, bright

    And precious and fair.

All praise be yours, my Lord, through Brothers Wind and Air,

    And fair and stormy, all the weather's moods,

    By which you cherish all that you have made.

All praise be yours, my Lord, through Sister Water,

    So useful, lowly, precious and pure.

All praise be yours, my Lord, through Brother Fire,

    Through whom you brighten up the night.

    How beautiful is he, how gay! Full of power and strength.

All praise be yours, my Lord, through Sister Earth, our mother,

    Who feeds us in her sovereignty and produces

    Various fruits with coloured flowers and herbs.[207]

These poetic lyrics indicate Francis's ability to rejoice in creation, in which he saw the reflection of God's goodness. He was filled with a joyful ecstasy when he beheld God's power in the sun, the moon, and the stars. Francis thought of Eternal Light when he saw a candle, and so he hesitated to blow it out. He thought of God the Rock when he stepped on stones, and so he tread upon them with reverence. Seeing God's beauty in meadows of flowers, in farm fields and vineyards, forests and fountains, gardens and all the rest, he preached to them as if they could hear him and respond, encouraging them to praise the Lord along with him.

We have many stories of this preaching, such as this one about a multitude of birds: When he approached the flock, the creatures appeared to listen, remaining perfectly still even as he walked among them. "My little bird sisters," he said to them, "you owe much to God your Creator, and you must always and everywhere praise Him."[208]

In all such things Francis was "carried away with joy and purest gladness," his earliest biographer reports.[209] Through God's "footprints impressed upon things," Francis "followed the Beloved everywhere; he made for himself from all things a ladder by which *to come even to his throne.*"[210]

Francis found in the things of earth a stairway to heaven. He was full of joy because he already tasted the sweetness of eternal bliss. He believed that the kingdom of God, just as Christ had said, was already present (see Matthew 10:7).

POPE FRANCIS AND JOY IN THE KINGDOM OF GOD

"The first word that I wish to say to you: *joy!* Do not be men and women of sadness: a Christian can never be sad!"[211]

Pope Francis spoke these words on his first Palm Sunday as pope. As he has shown in his own witness of joyful service to Christ throughout the years, this joy is not just an imaginary idea. It is one of the effects of our faith. "Joy is a sign of the Lord's presence," the pope has said.[212]

At a conference in 2007, Cardinal Jorge Bergoglio described his beautiful vision of Christian joy:

Dear friends, if we walk in hope, allowing ourselves to be surprised by the new wine which Jesus offers us, we have joy in our hearts and we cannot fail to be witnesses of this joy. Christians are joyful, they are never gloomy. God is at our side. We have a Mother who always intercedes for the life of her children, for us.... Jesus has shown us that the face of God is that of a loving Father. Sin and death have been defeated. Christians cannot be pessimists! They do not look like someone in constant mourning. If we are truly in love with Christ and if we sense how much he loves us, our heart will "light up" with a joy that spreads to everyone around us.[213]

The pope's understanding of Christian joy is thus twofold. First, as Christians we have reason to be joyful. And second, this joy should overflow into the world around us.

At the conference, he indicated that we have reason to rejoice because we are members of an amazing family! Mary is our mother. "Silent at the foot of the cross," taught Cardinal Bergoglio in 2008, "she heard the essence of her life: 'Behold your son.... Behold your children!' and from that moment she began still more to hold the people of God in her care."[214] We are blessed to be counted among the children of the Queen of Heaven herself. We benefit from her intercession and also learn from her example. As Pope Francis tells us, "Our Lady best transmits to the faithful the joy of God's word, which first filled her with pleasure."[215] Indeed Mary stands as a beautiful example because, as the Holy Father tells us, "her heart was filled with the joy of faith."[216]

And what can we expect as the children of a heavenly Father? "He doesn't promise riches or power," the cardinal said in 2005, "but what He does promise is His care and the greatest security you can find: refuge in the name of God. He promises His intimacy, the warmth of the Father, [and] His embrace, full of tenderness and understanding."[217]

And of Christ, who reigns now at the right hand of the Father, Pope Francis tells us, "Ours is not a joy born of having many possessions, but from having encountered a Person: Jesus, in our midst."[218] This person is Christ the King. He has won the victory over sin and death, thereby making us heirs to the kingdom that has no end.

But it is not enough to keep this joy to ourselves. The joy must overflow! We are called to go into the world and spread the joy of Christ to others. "Let us follow Jesus!" the Holy Father tells us. "We accompany, we follow Jesus, but above all we know that he accompanies us and carries us on his shoulders. This is our joy, this is the hope that we must bring to this world."[219]

After his first Easter Sunday Mass as pope, Francis joyfully exclaimed,

> Christ is risen! I would like it to go out to every house and every family, especially where the suffering is greatest, in hospitals, in prisons.... Most of all, I would like it to enter every heart, for it is there that God wants to sow this Good News: Jesus is risen, there is hope for you, you are no longer in the power of sin or of evil! Love has triumphed! Mercy has been victorious! God's mercy always triumphs.[220]

And it is clear that this pope—whether he is telling jokes in the middle of his homilies, mingling with the faithful after Mass, or grinning from ear to ear as he kisses babies—is filled with a captivating joy that flows out to the world. Indeed, Pope Francis believes that Christian service is misguided if it is not done in a spirit of joy. He exhorts priests:

> When there is joy in the heart of the pastor, it is a sign that his actions come from the Spirit.... It is not enough that our truth be orthodox and our pastoral action efficient. Without the joy of beauty, the truth becomes cold, even heartless and arrogant, as we see in the speech of many embittered fundamentalists. It is as if they were chewing on ashes instead of savoring the glorious sweetness of Christ's truth, which illuminates all of reality with a gentle glow.... Without the joy of beauty, any work for the good becomes a gloomy concern for efficiency, as it is for many overwhelmed activists. They go about clothing reality with mournful statistics instead of anointing it with the oil of inner gladness that transforms hearts, one by one, from within.[221]

One of the most natural places to encounter joy is in the presence of children. Pope Francis has clearly revealed his love for young people, and one has to wonder whether part of his affinity for the youth is his recognition of their inherent joy. In an archdiocesan Mass held especially for children in 2009, Cardinal Bergoglio encouraged them to radiate this joy to others:

> Listen well to this, so that there may be a celebration in each of your hearts: we must give joy to others, we must make others joyful, so that they arrive at the Feast of Jesus with open hearts. And this can be done. Each of us can make our companions, our brothers and sisters, our neighbors, our families, our friends, all of them, joyful. Each one of you,

each boy and girl, can bring joy to your friends and your families, each one of you can do good unto others.... The world is yours. Live within it in the light. And live in it with joy, because he who walks in the light has a joyful heart.[222]

And, as Christ himself has taught, we too are called to be like children. "Let the children come to me, and do not hinder them," the Lord said to his disciples, "for to such belongs the kingdom of God. Truly, I say to you, whoever does not receive the kingdom of God like a child shall not enter it" (Luke 18:16–17).

Indeed, we hope for nothing greater than to enter this heavenly kingdom. For, as Pope Francis tells us, our very goal as the people of God is to attain "the kingdom of God, which has been begun by God Himself on earth, and which is to be further extended until it is brought to perfection by Him at the end of time, when Christ, our life, shall appear (cf. Lumen Gentium, 9). The goal then is full communion with the Lord; it's to enter into his divine life where we will live the joy of his love without measure. That full joy."[223]

So let us rejoice with the children and with all the saints in glory. Forever and ever. Amen.

FOR REFLECTION: HOW WILL I RESPOND?

Catechism of the Catholic Church 736: "By this power of the Spirit, God's children can bear much fruit. He who has grafted us onto the true vine will make us bear 'the fruit of the Spirit:... love, joy, peace, patience, kindness, goodness, faithfulness, gentleness, self-control.' 'We live by the Spirit'; the more we renounce ourselves, the more we 'walk by the Spirit.'"

Consider: Am I bearing these fruits of the Spirit in my life? Which ones are most visible in my life? In particular, how do I reflect the joy of being one of God's children?

• • •

Pope Francis knows that following Christ means accepting the cross. But he also knows from personal experience that these burdens enable us to imitate Christ, and thus to find joy. So it was that the tremendous physical suffering from his lung infection was transformed when the future pope thought about imitating Christ. In such moments, he says we are called to "bear witness with cheerfulness."

Consider: What are the crosses in my life right now? How often do I unite them to the sufferings of Christ? How could I use them as opportunities to be a cheerful witness?

• • •

St. Francis saw God's footprints all around him. He viewed all of creation—people, animals, rocks, candles—as part of the glorious kingdom of God. And so he gave thanks to God with exuberant joy. As he told his sisters the birds, we should always and everywhere praise the Lord.

Consider: How often do I praise God for the gifts of creation? What things most help me experience the joy of the kingdom? Music? Art? Nature? Friendships? Learning? Children? How could I help others experience this joy?

NOTES

1. Francis of Assisi. "Testament of the Holy Father Saint Francis," in *The Writings of St. Francis of Assisi*, trans., Paschal Robinson (Philadelphia: Dolphin, 1905), http://www.sacred-texts.com/chr/wosf/wosf09.htm.

2. Pedro A. Moreno, O.P., "Faith Needs to be Shared!" *Sooner Catholic*, http://archokc.org/news/1960-column-faith-needs-to-be-shared.

3. Pope Leo XIII, "On St. Francis of Assisi," *Papal Encyclicals Online*, 14. http://www.papalencyclicals.net/Leo13/l13frc.htm.

4. G.K. Chesterton, *Saint Francis of Assisi* (New York: Image, 1990), pp. 15–16.

5. Chesterton, *Saint Francis of Assisi*, p. 56.

6. Pope Leo XIII, "On St. Francis of Assisi," 10.

7. Brian Bethune, "Suspension of Disbelief," Special Edition, *Maclean's* 126, no. 13 (April 8, 2013), pp. 16–27.

8. Pope Francis, "A Big Heart Open to God," interview by Antonio Spadaro, S.J., *America Magazine*, September 30, 2013. http://americamagazine.org/pope-interview.

9. Pope Francis, "A Big Heart Open to God."

10. "Cardinal Dolan Pope Francis Is 'Challenging Us,'" YouTube video, 3:46, from an interview on the *Today Show*, posted by Janet Marlboro, August 2, 2013, http://www.youtube.com/watch?v=vgo4hVnYElk.

11. Mark de Vries, "Christ, Christ Is the Centre," in *Caelo et in Terra* (blog), March 17, 2013. http://incaelo.wordpress.com/2013/03/17/christ-christ-is-the-centre/.

12. Pope Francis, "Full Text of Pope Francis's Address to Religious Leaders." Christian Churches Together, March 20, 2013, http://christianchurchestogether.org/full-text-of-pope-franciss-address-to-religious-leaders.

13. Jorge Mario Bergoglio, *In Him Alone Is Our Hope: The Church According to Pope Francis* (New York: Magnificat, 2013), p. 69.

14. Francis of Assisi, "Letter to All the Friars," in *The Writings of St. Francis of Assisi*.

15. Archbishop Jose H. Gomez, "Praying with Our New Pope," *The Tidings Online*, April 12, 2013, http://www.the-tidings.com/index.php/viewpoints/cardinals-archbishop-gomez/3321-praying-with-our-new-pope.

16. Thomas of Celano, "First and Second Life of St. Francis with selections from Treatise on the Miracles of Blessed Francis," in *Saint Francis of Assisi Writings and Early Biographies: English Omnibus of the Sources for the Life of St. Francis*, ed. Marion A. Habig (Cincinnati: Franciscan Media, 2008), pp. 246–247.

17. Francis of Assisi, *The Writings of Saint Francis*, in Habig, p. 33.

18. Francis of Assisi, *The Writings of Saint Francis*, in Habig, p. 38.

19. Omer Englebert, *St. Francis of Assisi: A Biography*, trans. Eve Marie Cooper (Cincinnati: Servant, 1979), p. 173.

20. Francis of Assisi, *The Writings of Saint Francis*, in Habig, p. 68.

21. Englebert, p. 156.

22. "Pope Francis," St. Ignatios of Antioch Melkite Catholic Church, http://www.melkite.net/who-we-are/our-clergy/pope-francis.

23. Rachel Donadio, "With Simple Actions and Dress, New Pope Shifts Tone at Vatican," *The New York Times*, March 14, 2013, http://www.nytimes.com/2013/03/15/world/europe/pope-francis.html?_r=0.

24. Pope Francis, Archdiocese of Miami, http://www.miamiarch.org/ipp.asp?op=Blog_1347171435507.

25. Francesca Ambrogetti and Sergio Rubin, *Pope Francis: His Life in His Own Words* (New York: Putnam, 2013), p. xxiv.

26. Francis of Assisi, *The Writings of Saint Francis*, in Habig, p. 36.

27. Francis of Assisi, *The Writings of Saint Francis*, in Habig, p. 37.

28. Francis of Assisi, *The Writings of Saint Francis*, in Habig, pp. 34–35.

29. Francis of Assisi, *The Writings of Saint Francis*, in Habig, p. 35.

30. *The Little Flowers of St. Francis*, chap. 3, www.ewtn.com.

31. *The Little Flowers of Saint Francis*, in Habig, p. 1376.

32. James Martin, S.J., "Final Vows? What's That?" *America Magazine*, October 30, 2009, http://americamagazine.org/content/all-things/final-vows-whats.

33. Carol Glatz, "Goodbye to Reading 'Boring' Text," *Catholic Herald*, June 13, 2013, p. 1, 11.

34. Pope Francis, "A Big Heart Open to God."

35. Thomas Craughwell, *Pope Francis: The Pope From the End of the Earth* (Charlotte, N.C.: Saint Benedict, 2013), pp. 166–167.

36. Robert Moynihan, *Pray for Me* (New York: Image, 2013), p. 122.

37. Moynihan, p. 24.

38. "A Surprise Call," Jesuits Missouri Province, http://www.jesuitsmissouri.org/act/newsShow.cfm?NewsID=88.

39. Moynihan, p. 23.
40. Moynihan, p. 26.
41. Moynihan, p. 207.
42. Ambrogetti and Rubin, *Pope Francis*, pp. 66–67.
43. Jorge Mario Bergoglio and Abraham Skorka, *On Heaven and Earth*, trans. Alejandro Bermudez and Howard Goodman, ed. Diego F. Rosemberg (New York: Image, 2013), p. 230.
44. Jean M. Heiman, "Pope Francis: True Power Comes with Service," *Catholic Fire* (blog). May 21, 2013, http://catholicfire.blogspot. com/2013/05/pope-francis-true-power-comes-with.html.
45. St. Francis, as quoted in "Reflections: St. Francis of Assisi," My Catholic Source, http://www.mycatholicsource.com/mcs/qt/saint_ francis_reflections_teachings_misc.htm.
46. Archbishop William E. Lori, *Chaplain's report 5*, no. 8 (August 2013), http://www.kofc.org/en/resources/chaplains/report8_13.pdf.
47. Agostino Ghilardi, *The Life and Times of St. Francis*, ed. Dr. Enzo Orlandi, trans. Salvator Attansio (Philadelphia: Curtis, 1967), p. 35.
48. Ghilardi, p. 35.
49. Englebert, p. 76.
50. Francis of Assisi, *The Writings of Saint Francis,* in Habig, p. 40.
51. Francis of Assisi, *The Writings of Saint Francis,* in Habig, p. 172.
52. Robert P. Imbelli, "Touching the Wounds of Jesus," *dotCommon-weal* (blog), *Commonweal Magazine*, July 3, 2013, https://www. commonwealmagazine.org/blog/touching-wounds-jesus.
53. Matthew E. Bunson, *Pope Francis* (Huntington, Ind.: Our Sunday Visitor, 2013), p. 146.
54. Dave Gibson, "The Church, a New Pope and People Living on Society's Margins – Why is St. Francis of Assisi a Model? Ways the Poor Evangelize Others," *Dave's Corner* (blog), March 31, 2013, http://www.jknirp.com/dave152.html.
55. Charles Dickens, *A Christmas Carol* (New York: Barnes and Noble, 1994), pp. 8–9.
56. Ambrogetti and Rubin, *Pope Francis*, pp. 258.
57. Pope Francis, Twitter post, June 4, 2013.
58. "Pope Francis Kind, Outspoken, a Good Administrator," Herald Malaysia Online, March 23, 2013, http://www.heraldmalaysia. com/news/Pope-Francis-kind,-outspoken,-a-good%20adminis-trator-14886-2-1.html.
59. Bergoglio and Skorka, *On Heaven and Earth*, p. 170.

60. Bergoglio and Skorka, *On Heaven and Earth*, pp. 168–169.

61. Thomas C. Fox, "Francis Speaks of Church Harmony, Service to the Poor," *National Catholic Reporter*, May 19, 2013, http://ncronline. org/blogs/ncr-today/francis-speaks-church-harmony-service-poor.

62. Rocco Palmo, "'You are Not Alone' – the 'Pope of the Slums' Returns to His Own," *Whispers in the Loggia* (blog), July 25, 2013, http://whispersintheloggia.blogspot.com/2013/07/you-are-not-alone-pope-of-slums-returns.html.

63. Christopher. "Pope to Buenos Aires: 'Instead of Going to Rome,'" *Jorge Mario Bergoglio Pope Francis* (blog), March 14, 2013, http:// pontificateofpopefrancis.blogspot.com/2013/03/pope to-buenos-aires-instead-of-going.html.

64. Chesterton, p. 47.

65. Francis of Assisi, *The Writings of Saint Francis*, in Habig, p. 76.

66. As quoted in Matthew Schmitz, "Pope Francis on How to Talk About Abortion, Gay Marriage, and Contraception," *First Things* (blog), September 20, 2013, http://www.firstthings.com/blogs/first-thoughts/2013/09/20/pope-francis-advice-on-how-to-talk-about-abortion-gay-marriage-and-contraception.

67. "Let Us Care for Life!" Pontifical Council for the Family, http://www.familiam.org/pls/pcpf/v3_s2ew_consultazione. mostra_paginawap?id_pagina=5012&attiva_menu=0&nohtml=0.

68. USCCB, USCCB to Michael Froman, July 19, 2013, http://www. usccb.org/issues-and-action/human-life-and-dignity/global-issues/ trade/upload/USTR-letter-7-19-13.pdf.

69. Bunson, *Pope Francis*, p. 187.

70. Bunson, *Pope Francis*, pp. 170–171.

71. Bergoglio and Skorka, *On Heaven and Earth*, p. 98.

72. Pope Francis, "A Big Heart Open to God."

73. Bunson, *Pope Francis*, p. 145.

74. Bunson, *Pope Francis*, pp. 154–155.

75. Bergoglio and Skorka, *On Heaven and Earth*, p. 171.

76. Rachel Zamarron, "When Did I See You Lord?" *Ignitum Today*, May 2, 2013, http://www.ignitumtoday.com/2013/05/02/ when-did-i-see-you-lord.

77. Bergoglio and Skorka, *On Heaven and Earth*, p. 162.

78. "Reflections: St. Francis of Assisi," My Catholic Source, http://www. mycatholicsource.com/mcs/qt/saint_francis_reflections_teachings_ misc.htm.

79. Joan Lewis, "The Church is the Body of Christ," *Joan's Rome* (blog), Eternal Word Television Network, June 19, 2013, http://www.ewtn.com/news/blog.asp?blogposts_ID=1759&blog_ID=1.
80. Pope Francis, "A Big Heart Open to God."
81. Englebert, p. 63.
82. Ghilardi, *The Life and Times of St. Francis*, p. 29.
83. Englebert, p. 129.
84. Englebert, p. 129.
85. Francis of Assisi, "Second Rule of the Friars Minor," In *The Writings of St. Francis*, http://www.sacred-texts.com/chr/wosf/wosf07.htm.
86. Francis of Assisi, *The Writings of Saint Francis*, in Habig, p. 33.
87. Francis of Assisi, *The Writings of Saint Francis*, in Habig, p. 44.
88. Francis of Assisi, *The Writings of Saint Francis*, in Habig, p. 46.
89. Englebert, p. 258.
90. Englebert, p. 264.
91. "Excerpts from the Interview with Pope Francis aboard the flight from World Youth Day in Rio de Janeiro to Rome." Catholic Hawaii.org, July 28, 2013, http://www.catholichawaii.org/media/224248/pope_francis_interview_on_rio-rome_flight_7-28-13.pdf.
92. Julie Schwietert Collazo and Lisa Rogak, eds., *Pope Francis: In His Own Words* (Novato, Calif.: New World Library, 2013), p. 20.
93. Moynihan, p. 152.
94. Ambrogetti and Rubin, *Pope Francis*, pp. 109–110.
95. Moynihan, p. 200.
96. Quoted in Sam Guzman, "Pope Francis: Pro-abortion Politicians Shouldn't Receive Communion," *Personally Speaking* (blog), Pro-Life Wisconsin, March 14, 2013, http://blog.prolifewisconsin.org/2013/03/14/pope-francis-pro-abortion-politicians-shouldnt-receive-communion.
97. Guzman, "Pope Francis: Pro-abortion Politicians."
98. Jorge Bergoglio, "Letter to the Carmelite Nuns of the Archdiocese of Buenos Aires," June 22, 2010, In *New Oxford Review*, May 1, 2013, p. 19.
99. Pope Francis, "A Big Heart Open to God."
100. Bishop John Michael Botean, "Easter Pastoral Letter 2013," Romanian Catholic Diocese Eparchy of St. George in Canton, April 3, 2013, http://www.romaniancatholic.org/2013/04/349.

101. Pope Francis, "A Big Heart Open to God."
102. Scott Landry, "Pope Francis greets and addresses the Media," *The Good Catholic Life*, March 17, 2013, http://www.thegoodcatholiclife.com/2013/03/17/pope-francis-greets-and-addresses-the-media/.
103. Rob Gasper, "Thank You, Pope Francis," American Life League, September 25, 2013, http://www.all.org/article/index/id/MTI1OTg.
104. Moynihan, p. 221.
105. St. Bonaventure, *Life of St. Francis*, as quoted by Pam Tremblay, "Francis, Rebuild My Church," *Ad Infinitum* (blog), Catholic Apostolate Center, March 14, 2013, http://www.catholicapostolate-center.org/1/post/2013/03/francis-rebuild-my-church.html.
106. Pope Leo XIII, "On St. Francis of Assisi," 8.
107. Pope Leo XIII, "On St. Francis of Assisi," 9.
108. Francis of Assisi, *The Writings of Saint Francis*, in Habig, p. 44.
109. Francis of Assisi, *The Writings of Saint Francis*, in Habig, p. 116.
110. Francis of Assisi, *The Writings of Saint Francis*, in Habig, p. 110.
111. Francis of Assisi, *The Writings of Saint Francis*, in Habig, p. 94–95.
112. Francis of Assisi, *The Writings of Saint Francis*, in Habig, p. 95–96.
113. Francis of Assisi, *The Writings of Saint Francis*, in Habig, p. 46.
114. Francis of Assisi, *The Writings of Saint Francis*, in Habig, p. 113.
115. St. Francis, "Testament," ewtn.com, emphasis added, www.ewtn.com/library/MARY/FRANTES.htm.
116. St. Bonaventure, *Lives of St. Francis*, in Habig, p. 699.
117. Fr. B. Jerabek, "Where Pope Francis Lives," Father Jerabek's Personal Blog, October 1, 2013, http://fatherjerabek.wordpress.com/2013/10/01/where-pope-francis-lives/comment-page-1.
118. Pope Francis, "A Big Heart Open to God."
119. Rocco Palmo, "'A Place of Mercy and Hope' – At Audience, Francis on 'Being Church,'" *Whispers in the Loggia*, June 12, 2013, http://whispersintheloggia.blogspot.com/2013/06/a-place-of-mercy-and-hope-at-audience.html.
120. Fr. B. Jerabek, "Where Pope Francis Lives."
121. Pope Francis, address to the College of Cardinals, March 15, 2013, quoted at Matthew Schmitz, "How Pope Francis Puts Spiritual Concepts in Today's Terms," *First Thoughts* (blog), First Things, May 9, 2013, http://www.firstthings.com/blogs/firstthoughts/2013/05/09/the-vivid-images-of-pope-francis.
122. Robert P. Imbelli, "Corpus Christi," *dotCommonweal* (blog), *Commonweal Magazine*, June 19, 2013, https://www.commonwealmagazine.org/blog/corpus-christi-0.

123. Pope Francis, Twitter post, August 11, 2013, https://twitter.com/Pontifex/status/366504281932693504.

124. Pope Francis, "Pope Francis' Weekly Catechesis," *Saint Joan of Arc*, June 12, 2013, http://www.saintjoan.org/index.php/catechesis.

125. Pope Francis, "Pope Francis' Weekly Catechesis," June 12, 2013.

126. Pope Francis, "Pope Francis' Weekly Catechesis," June 12, 2013.

127. Pope Francis, "Pope Francis' Weekly Catechesis," *Saint Joan of Arc*, June 19, 2013, http://www.saintjoan.org/index.php/catechesis.

128. Pope Francis, "Pope Francis' Weekly Catechesis," June 19, 2013.

129. Referencing Galatians 6:2.

130. Francis of Assisi, "Testament," in *The Writings of St. Francis of Assisi*.

131. "XXVIII World Youth Day." World Family of Radio Maria, March 24, 2013, http://www.radiomaria.org/wfm_Show.asp?LNG=FRA&KEY=10691&PRG=WFED.

132. "The Story Behind the Peace Prayer of St. Francis," www.franciscan-archive.org/patriarcha/peace.html.

133. St. Francis, "Letter to All the Faithful," in *The Writings of St. Francis*, p. 104.

134. St. Francis, "First Rule," in *The Writings of St. Francis*, p. 51.

135. Thomas of Celano, *Lives of St. Francis,* in Habig, p. 364.

136. St. Francis, "Canticle of the Sun," in *The Writings of St. Francis*, in Habig, p. 131.

137. Chesterton, p. 93.

138. "Words of Admonition of Our Holy Father St. Francis," in *The Writings of St. Francis of Assisi*, p.14.

139. Francis X. Rocca, "Pope, in Assisi, Calls on Church to Renounce 'Spirit of the World,'" *Catholic Herald* 145, no. 33, October 10, 2013, p. 7.

140. Hilarin Felder, *The Ideals of St. Francis of Assisi*, trans. Berchmans Bittle (New York: Benziger Brothers, 1925), p. 286.

141. Ghilardi, *Life and Times*, p. 37.

142. Francis of Assisi, *The Writings of Saint Francis,* in Habig, p. 60.

143. Felder, *The Ideals of St. Francis*, p. 284.

144. Francis of Assisi, *The Writings of St. Francis of Assisi*, p. 284.

145. "Sheet Which St. Francis Gave Brother Leo," in *The Writings of St. Francis of Assisi*, p. 149.

146. Pope Francis, "A Big Heart Open to God."

147. Christina Fernandez de Kirchner as quoted by Rachel Donadio and Alan Cowell, "Pope Francis Meets with Argentine Leader," *The Columbus Dispatch*, March 19, 2013, http://www.dispatch.com/content/stories/national_world/2013/03/19/pope-meets-with-argentine-leader.html.

148. Bergoglio, *In Him Alone Is Our Hope*, p. 115.

149. Bergoglio, *In Him Alone Is Our Hope*, p. 115.

150. Bergoglio, *In Him Alone Is Our Hope*, p. 115.

151. Bergoglio, *In Him Alone Is Our Hope*, pp. 114–115.

152. Bergoglio, *In Him Alone Is Our Hope*, p. 114.

153. Bergoglio, *In Him Alone Is Our Hope*, p. 114.

154. Bergoglio, *In Him Alone Is Our Hope*, p. 44.

155. Bergoglio, *In Him Alone Is Our Hope*, p. 115.

156. Pope Francis, *Encountering Christ: Homilies, Letters, and Addresses of Cardinal Jorge Bergoglio* (New Rochelle, N.Y.: Scepter, 2013), p. 41.

157. Bergoglio, *In Him Alone Is Our Hope*, p. 82.

158. "Message of the Year of Faith," as quoted in Pope Francis, *Encountering Christ*, p. 3.

159. Bergoglio, *In Him Alone Is Our Hope*, p. 116.

160. Francis of Assisi, *The Writings of St. Francis*, in Habig, p. 41.

161. Thomas of Celano, quoted in Habig, p. 451.

162. Dietrich von Hildebrand, *Image of Christ: Saint Francis of Assisi* (Steubenville: Franciscan University Press, 1993), p. 81.

163. Hildebrand, *Image of Christ*, p. 82.

164. Felder, *The Ideals of St. Francis*, p. 292.

165. Bunson, *Pope Francis*, p. 136.

166. Bunson, *Pope Francis*, p. 135.

167. Ambrogetti and Rubin, *Pope Francis*, p. xxvi.

168. "Pope Francis Convokes Day of Prayer and Penance for Peace in the Middle East on September 7," *E-Scroll* (blog), Diocese of Orlando, August 30, 2013, http://www.orlandodiocese.org/e-scroll-current-issue/item/19149-pope-francis-convokes-day-of-prayer-and-penance-for-peace-in-the-middle-east-on-september-7.

169. "Pope Francis Convokes Day of Prayer and Penance for Peace in the Middle East on September 7."

170. SBrinkmann, "Thousands fill St. Peter's Square for Prayer Vigil," *WOGBlog*, Women of Grace, September 11, 2013, http://www.womenofgrace.com/blog/?p=24082.

171. SBrinkmann, "Thousands fill St. Peter's Square."

172. "Genuine Dialogue," The Politicus, http://www.thepoliticus.com/category/main-topics/genuine-dialogue.
173. Bergoglio and Skorka, *On Heaven and Earth*, pp. xiv–xv.
174. Craughwell, *Pope Francis*, p. 138.
175. *The Legend of Perugia*, in Habig, p. 1074.
176. Francis X. Rocca, "Pope Denounces 'Poison' of Consumerism in 'Society Based on Profit," CatholicPhilly.com, August 5, 2013, http://catholicphilly.com/2013/08/us-world-news/world-catholic-news/pope-denounces-poison-of-consumerism-in-society-based-on-profit.
177. Bosco Peters, "Sede Occupata," *Liturgy*, March 15, 2013, http://liturgy.co.nz/sede-occupata/14216.
178. Chiara Frugoni, *Francis of Assisi: A Life* (New York: Continuum, 1998), p. 119.
179. Frugoni, p. 119.
180. Frugoni, p. 125.
181. Julien Green, *God's Fool: The Life and Times of Francis of Assisi* (San Francisco: Harper and Row, 1983), p. 255.
182. Francis of Assisi, *The Writings of St. Francis*, in Habig, p. 45.
183. Francis of Assisi, *The Writings of St. Francis*, in Habig, pp. 40–41.
184. *Legend of the Three Companions*, in Habig, p. 928.
185. *Legend of the Three Companions*, in Habig, p. 912.
186. Chesterton, pp. 103–104.
187. Authors' paraphrase based on Ghilardi, *Life and Times*, p. 32.
188. Ambrogetti and Rubin, *Pope Francis*, p. 23.
189. Ambrogetti and Rubin, *Pope Francis*, p. 24.
190. Ambrogetti and Rubin, *Pope Francis*, p. 25.
191. Moynihan, p. 221.
192. Ambrogetti and Rubin, *Pope Francis*, pp. 27–28.
193. Joan Lewis, "Tweets from Pope Francis – Good Christians Don't Constantly Complain, They are Joyful and Patient," *Joan's Rome* (blog), Eternal Television Network, May 7, 2013, http://www.ewtn.com/news/blog.asp?blogposts_ID=1726&blog_ID=1.
194. Ambrogetti and Rubin, *Pope Francis*, p. 28.
195. Ambrogetti and Rubin, *Pope Francis*, p. 24.
196. Cardinal Donald Wuerl, "The Grace and Courage to Lay Down One's Life for Christ," *Seek First the Kingdom* (blog), March 26, 2013, http://cardinalsblog.adw.org/2013/03/the-grace-and-courage-to-lay-down-ones-life-for-christ.
197. Moynihan, *Pray for Me*, p. 193.
198. Ambrogetti and Rubin, *Pope Francis*, p. 194.
199. Pope Francis, Twitter post, July 10, 2013, https://twitter.com/Pontifex/status/354890430216810497.

200. Englebert, p. 26.
201. Thomas of Celano, *First and Second Life of St. Francis*, in Habig, p. 242.
202. Francis of Assisi, *The Writings of St. Francis*, in Habig, p. 38.
203. Oligny, "Legend of Perugia," p. 1074.
204. Thomas of Celano, *First and Second Life of St. Francis*, in Habig, pp. 465–466, quoting Psalm 50:14.
205. *The Mirror of Perfection*, in Habig, p. 1236.
206. Ghilardi, *Life and Times*, p. 68.
207. Francis of Assisi, *The Writings of St. Francis*, in Habig, pp. 130–132.
208. *Little Flowers of St. Francis*, in Habig, p. 1336.
209. Thomas of Celano, *First and Second Life of St. Francis*, in Habig, pp. 296–297.
210. Thomas of Celano, *First and Second Life of St. Francis*, in Habig, p. 495, quoting Job 23:3.
211. "A Christian Can Never Be Sad," *Ad Infinitum* (blog), Catholic Apostolate Center, May 30, 2013, http://www.catholicapostolate-center.org/1/post/2013/05/a-christian-can-never-be-sad.html.
212. Bergoglio, *In Him Alone Is Our Hope*, p. 85.
213. "From Pope Francis in Brazil This Week," Church of St. Lawrence O'Toole, July 26, 2013, http://www.stlawrenceotoole.org/node/2931.
214. Moynihan, p. 190.
215. Collazo and Rogak, *Pope Francis*, p. 86.
216. Luca Rolandi, "Francis: Mary helps us undo painful knots in our lives," *Vatican Insider*, Oct 12, 2013, http://vaticaninsider.lastampa.it/en/the-vatican/detail/articolo/vaticano-vatican-maria-mary-28561.
217. Collazo and Rogak, *Pope Francis*, pp. 38–39.
218. "A Christian Can Never Be Sad."
219. "A Christian Can Never Be Sad."
220. Mark Zimmerman, "In Pope Francis' Words, Now 'Go Out' and Share the Risen Christ," *Editor's Notebook* (blog), My Catholic Standard, Archdiocese of Washington, April 1, 2013, http://cathstan.org/main.asp?SectionID=65&SubSectionID=192&ArticleID=5613&TM=58992.41.
221. Pope Francis, *Encountering Christ*, pp. 104–105.
222. Moynihan, p. 222.
223. Pope Francis, "Pope Francis' Weekly Catechesis," June 12, 2013.

A Note from the Authors

During the course of our work on this manuscript, we were blessed to be able to make a pilgrimage to Rome together as father and daughter. The highlight of this trip was our participation in a private audience with Pope Francis. At the end of the audience, contrary to the established plan, the pope took time to greet all 150 of us in person. What a joy it was to stand before the real man about whom we had been learning and writing for months! We were both impressed by his warmth, his kindness, and his humility. He greeted us with focused attention, and he took special time to kiss and bless Gina's baby who traveled with us. We left the audience quite moved by the encounter with our Holy Father, who truly seemed to care about each and every one of us there present. We hope that our book will convey, in some small way, the essence of this man who has so generously embraced the mission to care for us all.